50 State Step by Step Guide to Forming Nonprofit Charitable Organization

What Forms To Fill Out, How & Where To File, The Exact Cost For Filing, What Licenses And Permits You Need For Each State

By

Aaron Sanders

Copyrighted Material

*Copyright © 2018 – **Lost River Publishing House***

All Rights Reserved.

No part of this publication may be reproduced, stored in a retrieval system or transmitted in any form or by any means, electronic, mechanical, photocopying, recording or otherwise without the proper written consent of the copyright holder, except as permitted under Sections 107 & 108 of the 1976 United States Copyright Act, without the prior written permission of the publisher.

Limited of Liability & Disclaimer of Warranty: The publisher and the author make no representations or warranties with respect to the accuracy or completeness of the contents of this book and specifically disclaim all warranties including warranties of fitness for any specific or particular purpose. Lost River Publishing House publishes its books and guides in a variety of electronic and print formats, Some content that appears in print may not be available in electronic format, and vice versa.

Cover design

Robin Goodnight

First Edition

TABLE OF CONTENTS

Foreword 6
How to Use this Guide 7
    Naming and/or registering your business name 7
    Articles of Incorporation 7
    Registered Agent 7
    EIN from IRS 8
    Filing for 501 © Status 8
    Initial Governing Policies and Documents 8
    State Tax number and Exemption 9
    Charitable Solicitation Registration 9
    Business Licenses and Permits 9
Alabama 11
Alaska 18
Arizona 24
Arkansas 30
California 37
Colorado 45
Connecticut 52
Delaware 58
District of Columbia 64
Florida 71
Georgia 77
Hawaii 83
Idaho 89
Illinois 94
Indiana 101
Iowa 107
Kansas 112
Kentucky 119
Louisiana 125
Maine 132

Maryland	139
Massachusetts	146
Michigan	152
Minnesota	158
Mississippi	165
Missouri	171
Montana	177
Nebraska	182
Nevada	187
New Hampshire	194
New Jersey	200
New Mexico	206
New York	212
North Carolina	219
North Dakota	225
Ohio	231
Oklahoma	237
Oregon	243
Pennsylvania	249
Rhode Island	256
South Carolina	262
South Dakota	268
Tennessee	274
Texas	280
Utah	286
Vermont	292
Virginia	297
Washington	304
West Virginia	310
Wisconsin	317
Wyoming	324
Appendix – 1	329
Sample Articles of Incorporation	329

- Appendix – 2 333
  - Sample Conflict of Interest Polices 333
  - ACKNOWLEDGMENT AND FINANCIAL INTEREST DISCLOSURE STATEMENT 341

FOREWORD

This guide is intended for people who are about to start a nonprofit organization and wants to find out the exact steps they need to take to get started. This is not a guide where I discuss what a nonprofit organization does or its purpose. If you need to learn more about the basic operation of a nonprofit organization and how to get started, you can look up my other book "How to start, Run & Grow a Successful Nonprofit Organization."

In this guide, I outlined every step you need to take to get started with your nonprofit for your specific state including the most up to date filing costs for all 50 states including the District of Columbia.

As the requirements and filing fees change, I will update them accordingly.

At the end of this guide, you will find samples of two very important documents.

- A Sample Conflict of Interest Policy Statement
- A Sample Articles of Incorporation

Good luck on your new NPO. I wish you all the success.

HOW TO USE THIS GUIDE

For each and every state I outlined 13-14 steps that one needs to take to start a NPO successfully. Since some of the steps are same for all 50 states, I decided to explain those basic steps so you will have a clear understanding as to what and how to accomplish them.

NAMING AND/OR REGISTERING YOUR BUSINESS NAME

The best way to do this step is to come up with at least 5-6 names first. Then go on to your State's Secretary of State's website, go into the business services section, and you will see a name search/reserve option. Run the previously chosen names to see which one of those are available for you to register. Once you find the best name for your business that is still available, go ahead and reserve it.

ARTICLES OF INCORPORATION

Every business that is incorporated needs its articles of incorporation. It is a simple document that details out what your company's purpose is, what your nature of business is along with who owns this entity. Typically you will need an attorney to create one of these documents for you. But if you are a small business, you can easily go on to one of the many online legal help sites like Legalzoom.com or lawdepot.com, etc. there are many great reputable sites that offer this service for a small fee.

REGISTERED AGENT

In most states, if you are trying to open a business or trying to incorporate your business, you need a physical presence in that state. In the event you do not reside in the state you are trying to open a business in, you then have to assign someone as the registered agent to act on your behalf.

EIN FROM IRS

Every business needs an Employer Identification Number (EIN) from the IRS. It is essentially like the social security number for your business. This is one of the most crucial and must complete step for your business. It is very easy to obtain. You can either have your CPA or accountant apply for it, or you can go on IRS's website and apply for this number.
Here is a link to IRS site where you can apply.

https://www.irs.gov/businesses/small-businesses-self-employed/apply-for-an-employer-identification-number-ein-online

FILING FOR 501 © STATUS

In this step, you have to file and be granted a tax-exempt status by the IRS, for this you will need to fill out IRS form 1023, form 1023-EZ or form 1024 depending on your organization's purpose. My advice is get help from a CPA or an accountant to get this done.

INITIAL GOVERNING POLICIES AND DOCUMENTS

There are two more important documents that you will need to create either by your attorney, or you can have them done by one of the online legal help sites like I mentioned before.

A. The Bylaws
B. A Solid Conflict of Interest Policy

The bylaws are essentially the operating agreement for your nonprofit organization. This is where you outline how the company operates, how often the directors of the board meet, how the records are kept and such.

Conflict of interest policy is another vital document for each and every nonprofit organization because this is where you have to detail out if there are any conflicts of interest between the employees, board members or directors and your organization's ordinary course of business.

Please look at the end of this book for a sample conflict of interest document.

STATE TAX NUMBER AND EXEMPTION

Once you have your IRS determination letter (501 C granted), you need to visit your local state's revenue department to obtain a tax ID number and a tax-exempt certificate. But the requirements and steps vary widely from state to state, so follow the instruction I provided in this guide for your state.

CHARITABLE SOLICITATION REGISTRATION

This is yet another area where it varies widely between states, but most require it on an annual basis. This mean you need to register and renew with your state every year before fundraising from any resident of the state. Depending on the scope of your organization you may need to register in other states as well. Follow this guide to find out where you need to register for your state.

BUSINESS LICENSES AND PERMITS

In addition to what I outlined so far, you will also need a few city, county, and state licenses and or permits again depending on where you live. Follow this guide to learn what licenses and permits you need for your state.

Annual Renewals:

Most businesses are typically required to renew their business licenses and permits annually, and your NPO is no exceptions. I outlined what licenses and permits you need to renew for your state every year.

ALABAMA

Step-1: Name Your Nonprofit

The name of your nonprofit will establish its brand and will allow you to incorporate with the state. The name you choose cannot conflict with any other organization registered within the state of Alabama. Make sure the name you choose is available and meets all state requirements. Search through the Alabama Secretary of State - Business Services Division.

Step-2: Reserve a Name

A name reservation is required in the state of Alabama:

Form: Name Reservation Request Form for Domestic Entities
Submit To: Alabama Secretary of State
Web Address: https://www.alabamainteractive.org/sos/introduction_input.action
How to File: Mail, courier or online. State of Alabama does not accept fax or email
Cost: $10 for mail processing, $25 for mail processing less than 3 days, $28 for online 24-hour processing
Time Frame: Standard mail is processed in order received, expedited mail is less than 3 days and online is less than 24 hours.

Additional Notes:
- You will be issued a Name Reservation Certificate that needs to be submitted with your Certificate of Formation
- Any names that have a professional designation in them will require proof of licensing.

Step-3: Get Initial Directors and Incorporators

The incorporate is the individual who signs the Articles of Incorporation for your business. You will need at least one incorporator, but you can have additional. The directors are the governing body of your nonprofit and are stakeholders in the purpose and success of your nonprofit. You should have at least three directors who are unrelated individuals in order to meet IRS requirements. You'll also want to meet age and residency requirements.

Step-4: Selected a Registered Agent

The registered agent is always responsible for receiving legal notices for your nonprofit. A registered agent needs to be physically living in the state and maintain an office open during regular business hours.

Step-5: Articles of Incorporation

The articles of incorporation are the official creation of your nonprofit. They show where and when the nonprofit was formed and provide the necessary information to verify the nonprofits existence. Make sure your articles of incorporation meet state and IRS requirement.

Form: Domestic Nonprofit Corporation Certificate of Formation
Submit To: Alabama Secretary of State - Business Services Division
How to File: Mail
Cost: $100 filing fee + $50 minimum county filing fee
Time Frame: About 3-5 days

Additional Notes:
- Send one original and two signed copies to the Office of the Judge of Probate in your county.
- Attach a Name Reservation Certificate

Step-6: Get an Employer Identification Number (EIN)

This is a unique nine-digit number that the IRS assigned to identify your nonprofit. Your EIN is then used to open a bank account, apply for 501(c)(3) status and submit 990 IRS returns.

Form: IRS Form SS-4
Submit To: Internal Revenue Service (IRS)
How to File: Mail, phone, fax or online
Cost: $0
Time Frame: By phone or online is immediate, by fax is 4 days and by mail is 4-5 weeks.

Additional Notes:
- Print EIN before closing session

Step-7: Storing Records

As you start a nonprofit, you will be faced with a number of official documents. Be sure you organize and store all of these records together for easy access later.

Step-8: Initial Governing Policies and Documents

The governing document for your nonprofit is your bylaws since they serve as the operating manual for your organization and need to be consistent with both the law and your articles of incorporation. The first meeting of your Board of Directors should be to review and ratify the bylaws.

You should also create and adopt a conflict of interest policy. This will guide you in what to do if someone in a key position within your nonprofit has competing interests and makes decision that benefit themselves while harming your nonprofit. Organizational interests should be prioritized ahead of personal interests. All conflicts should be disclosed immediately.

Both the bylaws and the conflict of interest policy will need to be approved and adopted before applying to the IRS for 501(c)(3) status.

Step-9: Board of Directors Organizational Meeting

This initial meeting is the most productive and important one. You will approve bylaws, adopt the conflict of interest policy, elect directors, appoint officers and approve any resolutions like opening a bank account. Be sure to record the decisions made in meeting minutes.

Alabama required a minimum of three days' notice for this initial meeting.

Step-10: State Tax Identification Numbers and Accounts

Incorporating a nonprofit means, you will follow all state laws. Requirements vary by state so check with your individual state first.

Alabama has a consolidated state tax registration application:

Form: COM-101: Alabama Department of Revenue Combined Registration/Application
Submit To: Alabama Department of Revenue
How to File: Mail or online
Cost: $0
Time Frame: About 3-5 days online
Step-11: File for 501(c) Status

This can seem like one of the most difficult steps in starting your nonprofit, but it also offers many benefits. After applying and submitting your documents, the IRS will give you a Determination Letter that officially recognizes your tax-exempt status.

Form: IRS Form 1023, Form 1023-EZ or Form 1024
Submit To: Internal Revenue Service (IRS)
How to File: Mail
Cost: $275 for Form 1023-EZ and $600 for Form 1023
Time Frame: Less than a month for Form 1023-EZ and 3-6 months for Form 1023

Step-12: State Tax Exemption

Once you have your IRS Determination Letter, you next need to figure out your state's requirements for tax-exempt status. This is another area that varies by state. You may also need to do periodic renewals for tax-exempt status.

In Alabama, you obtain your state income tax exemption when you get your IRS Determination Letter.

For state sales tax exemption in Alabama you need to do the following:

Form: ST: EX-A1: Application for Sales Tax Certificate of Exemption and Instructions
Submit To: Alabama Department of Revenue
Cost: $0

Additional Notes:
- In Alabama, most nonprofits won't qualify for sales tax exemption with a few exceptions.

Step-13: Charitable Solicitation Registration

This is yet another area where it varies between states, but most require it on an annual basis. This mean you need to register with the state before fundraising from any resident of the state. Depending on the scope of your organization you many need to register in other states as well.

Overseen By: Alabama Attorney General - Consumer Interest Division

Exemptions:

1. Less than $25,000 contributions nationwide in a fiscal year
2. Religious organizations
3. Educational institutions
4. Political organizations
5. Fraternal organizations
6. Civic leagues and organizations
7. Appeals for individuals under $10,000

To file in Alabama, you need to do the following:

Form: Charitable Organization Registration Form (URS)
Submit To: Alabama Attorney General - Consumer Interest Division
How to File: Mail or online
Cost: $25

Additional Notes:

- Attach all necessary documents
- Must be signed by the CFO and President or other authorized officer
- Signatures must be notarized

Step-14: Business Licenses and Permits

From here you will be all set to start your nonprofit. However, the work isn't over yet. You'll also need to stay in compliance with your nonprofit. Next, consider your required annual filings to remain legal.

Annual Renewal

1. IRS Renewals
    a. IRS Form 990
    b. Due the 15th day of the 5th month following the end of the taxable year.
2. Alabama has no renewal requirements for corporate income tax exemption.
3. Alabama Sales Tax Exemption Renewal
    a. Filed with the Alabama Department of Revenue
    b. Due annually
    c. Date of renewal is on current exemption certificate
4. Alabama doesn't require an annual report.
5. Charitable Solicitation Renewal
    a. Filed with the Alabama Attorney General - Consumer Interest Division
    b. Form URS plus your IRS Form 990 or your financial statements
    c. Filed by mail
    d. Costs $25
    e. Renewal is annually within 90 days of the close of the fiscal year
    f. Must be signed by the CFO and the President or other authorized officer
    g. Signatures must be notarized
    h. Any change in information during the 90 days must be reported to the attorney general
    i. File a Charitable Organization Notice of Non-Renewal if you don't want to renew.

ALASKA

Step-1: Name Your Nonprofit

The name of your nonprofit will establish its brand and will allow you to incorporate with the state. The name you choose cannot conflict with any other organization registered within the state of Alaska. Make sure the name you choose is available and meets all state requirement. Search through the Alaska Division of Corporations, Business and Professional Licensing.

Step-2: Get Initial Directors and Incorporators

The incorporate is the individual who signs the Articles of Incorporation for your business. You will need at least one incorporator, but you can have additional. The directors are the governing body of your nonprofit and are stakeholders in the purpose and success of your nonprofit. You should have at least three directors who are unrelated individuals in order to meet IRS requirements. You'll also want to meet age and residency requirements.

Step-3: Selected a Registered Agent

The registered agent is responsible for receiving legal notices for your nonprofit. A registered agent needs to be physically living in the state and maintain an office open during regular business hours.

Step-4: Articles of Incorporation

The articles of incorporation are the official creation of your nonprofit. They show where and when the nonprofit was formed and provide the necessary information to verify the

nonprofits existence. Make sure your articles of incorporation meet state and IRS requirement.

Form: Articles of Incorporation
Submit To: Alaska Division of Corporations, Business and Professional Licensing
How to File: Mail or online
Cost: $50
Time Frame: About 10-15 days by mail. Immediate online.
Additional Notes:
- The articles of incorporation can include a provision that will limit or eliminate the personal liability of a director for monetary damages as a result of the breach of fiduciary duty as a director.
- Submit two copies of your articles of incorporation.
- After approval, one copy will be stamped "filed" with the date and kept in the commissioner's office. The other copy is returned to you with an attached certificate of incorporation.

Step-5: Get an Employer Identification Number (EIN)

This is a unique nine-digit number that the IRS assigned to identify your nonprofit. Your EIN is then used to open a bank account, apply for 501(c)(3) status and submit 990 IRS returns.

Form: IRS Form SS-4
Submit To: Internal Revenue Service (IRS)
How to File: Mail, phone, fax or online
Cost: $0
Time Frame: By phone or online is immediate, by fax is 4 days and by mail is 4-5 weeks.

Additional Notes:

- Print EIN before closing session

Step-6: Storing Records

As you start a nonprofit, you will be faced with a number of official documents. Be sure you organize and store all of these records together for easy access later.

Step-7: Initial Governing Policies and Documents

The governing document for your nonprofit is your bylaws since they serve as the operating manual for your organization and need to be consistent with both the law and your articles of incorporation. The first meeting of your Board of Directors should be to review and ratify the bylaws.

You should also create and adopt a conflict of interest policy. This will guide you in what to do if someone in a key position within your nonprofit has competing interests and makes decision that benefit themselves while harming your nonprofit. Organizational interests should be prioritized ahead of personal interests. All conflicts should be disclosed immediately.

Both the bylaws and the conflict of interest policy will need to be approved and adopted before applying to the IRS for 501(c)(3) status.

Step-8: Board of Directors Organizational Meeting

This initial meeting is the most productive and important one. You will approve bylaws, adopt the conflict of interest policy, elect directors, appoint officers and approve any resolutions like opening a bank account. Be sure to record the decisions made in meeting minutes.

Alaska requires a minimum of three days' notice for this initial meeting.

Step-9: State Tax Identification Numbers and Accounts

Incorporating a nonprofit means, you will follow all state laws. Requirements vary by state so check with your individual state first.

Alaska does not offer a consolidated state tax registration application. This means you need to apply for each tax account you need. Check with the Alaska Department of Revenue for your nonprofits specific requirements.

Step-10: File for 501(c) Status

This can seem like one of the most difficult steps in starting your nonprofit, but it also offers many benefits. After applying and submitting your documents, the IRS will give you a Determination Letter that officially recognizes your tax-exempt status.

Form: IRS Form 1023, Form 1023-EZ or Form 1024
Submit To: Internal Revenue Service (IRS)
How to File: Mail
Cost: $275 for Form 1023-EZ and $600 for Form 1023
Time Frame: Less than a month for Form 1023-EZ and 3-6 months for Form 1023

Step-11: State Tax Exemption

Once you have your IRS Determination Letter, you next need to figure out your state's requirements for tax-exempt status. This is another area that varies by state. You may also need to do periodic renewals for tax-exempt status.
In Alaska, you obtain your state income tax exemption when you get your IRS Determination Letter.

Alaska doesn't have a state-level sales tax.

Step-12: Charitable Solicitation Registration

This is yet another area where it varies between states, but most require it on an annual basis. This mean you need to register with the state before fundraising from any resident of the state. Depending on the scope of your organization you many need to register in other states as well.

Overseen By: Alaska Department of Law - Consumer Protection Unit

Exemptions:
1. Less than $5,000 national contributions in a fiscal year or less than 10 donors in a fiscal year. For this exemption, you need to maintain financial records for 5 years.
2. Religious organizations
3. Political groups or candidates

To file in Alaska, you need to do the following:

Form: Alaska Charitable Organization Annual Registration Form
Submit To: Alaska Department of Law - Consumer Protection Unit
How to File: Mail, fax or online
Cost: $40

Additional Notes:
- Attach all necessary documents
- One authorized signature is required
- Signatures must be notarized

Step-13: Business Licenses and Permits

From here you will be all set to start your nonprofit. However, the work isn't over yet. You'll also need to stay in compliance with your nonprofit. Next, consider your required annual filings to remain legal.

Annual Renewal

1. IRS Renewals
    a. IRS Form 990
    b. Due the 15th day of the 5th month following the end of the taxable year.
2. Alaska has no renewal requirements for corporate income tax exemption.
3. Alaska has no sales tax.
4. File a Alaska Biennial Report
    a. File with the Alaska Division of Corporations, Business and Professional Licensing
    b. File by mail or online
    c. Cost $25 for nonprofit corporations or religious organizations. $100 for cooperative corporations
    d. Processed immediately online and about 10-15 days by mail
    e. If filed after August 1st there is a $5 late fee
5. Charitable Solicitation Renewal
    a. Filed with the Alaska Department of Law - Consumer Protection Unit
    b. Alaska Charitable Organization Annual Registration Form
    c. Filed by mail, fax or online
    d. Costs $40
    e. Renewal is annually by August 31st
    f. Include all necessary files including an annual financial report
    g. No late fee, but you aren't authorized to solicit until you get renewed

ARIZONA

Step-1: Name Your Nonprofit

The name of your nonprofit will establish its brand and will allow you to incorporate with the state. The name you choose cannot conflict with any other organization registered within the state of Arizona. Make sure the name you choose is available and meets all state requirement. Search through the Arizona Corporation Commission - Corporations Division.

Step-2: Get Initial Directors and Incorporators

The incorporate is the individual who signs the Articles of Incorporation for your business. You will need at least one incorporator, but you can have additional. The directors are the governing body of your nonprofit and are stakeholders in the purpose and success of your nonprofit. You should have at least three directors who are unrelated individuals in order to meet IRS requirements. You'll also want to meet age and residency requirements.

Step-3: Selected a Registered Agent

The registered agent is responsible for receiving legal notices for your nonprofit. A registered agent needs to be physically living in the state and maintain an office open during regular business hours.

Step-4: Articles of Incorporation

The articles of incorporation are the official creation of your nonprofit. They show where and when the nonprofit was formed and provide the necessary information to verify the

nonprofits existence. Make sure your articles of incorporation meet state and IRS requirement.

Form: Articles of Incorporation - Nonprofit
Submit To: Arizona Corporation Commission - Corporations Division
How to File: Mail or in person
Cost: $40 + optional $35 expedite
Time Frame: About 2 months. About 7-10 days if expedited

Additional Notes:
- A completed application needs to be accompanied by the following:
    - Form CFCVLR: Cover Sheet
    - Form CF0041: Articles of Incorporation
    - Form C082: Director Attachment
    - Form C084: Incorporator Attachment
    - Form M002: Statutory Agent Acceptance
    - Form CF0001: Certificate of Disclosure
    - Payment

Step-5: Publish Your Incorporation

In Arizona, a new nonprofit is required to publish in the county where your business is within 60 days and for 3 consecutive publications.

Step-6: Get an Employer Identification Number (EIN)

This is a unique nine-digit number that the IRS assigned to identify your nonprofit. Your EIN is then used to open a bank account, apply for 501(c)(3) status and submit 990 IRS returns.

Form: IRS Form SS-4
Submit To: Internal Revenue Service (IRS)
How to File: Mail, phone, fax or online
Cost: $0
Time Frame: By phone or online is immediate, by fax is 4 days and by mail is 4-5 weeks.

Additional Notes:
- Print EIN before closing session

Step-7: Storing Records

As you start a nonprofit, you will be faced with a number of official documents. Be sure you organize and store all of these records together for easy access later.

Step-8: Initial Governing Policies and Documents

The governing document for your nonprofit is your bylaws since they serve as the operating manual for your organization and need to be consistent with both the law and your articles of incorporation. The first meeting of your Board of Directors should be to review and ratify the bylaws.

You should also create and adopt a conflict of interest policy. This will guide you in what to do if someone in a key position within your nonprofit has competing interests and makes decision that benefit themselves while harming your nonprofit. Organizational interests should be prioritized ahead of personal interests. All conflicts should be disclosed immediately.

Both the bylaws and the conflict of interest policy will need to be approved and adopted before applying to the IRS for 501(c)(3) status.

Step-9: Board of Directors Organizational Meeting

This initial meeting is the most productive and important one. You will approve bylaws, adopt the conflict of interest policy, elect directors, appoint officers and approve any resolutions like opening a bank account. Be sure to record the decisions made in meeting minutes.

Step-10: State Tax Identification Numbers and Accounts

Incorporating a nonprofit means, you will follow all state laws. Requirements vary by state so check with your individual state first.

Arizona does not have a consolidated state tax application so you'll need to apply for each tax account you need:

Form: JT-1: Arizona Joint Tax Application Form
Submit To: Arizona Department of Revenue
Cost: $12 per license and location

Step-11: File for 501(c) Status

This can seem like one of the most difficult steps in starting your nonprofit, but it also offers many benefits. After applying and submitting your documents, the IRS will give you a Determination Letter that officially recognizes your tax-exempt status.

Form: IRS Form 1023, Form 1023-EZ or Form 1024
Submit To: Internal Revenue Service (IRS)
How to File: Mail
Cost: $275 for Form 1023-EZ and $600 for Form 1023
Time Frame: Less than a month for Form 1023-EZ and 3-6 months for Form 1023
Step-12: State Tax Exemption

Once you have your IRS Determination Letter, you next need to figure out your state's requirements for tax-exempt status. This is another area that varies by state. You may also need to do periodic renewals for tax-exempt status.

In Arizona, you obtain your state income tax exemption when you get your IRS Determination Letter.

For transaction privilege tax exemption in Arizona, you need to contact the Arizona Department of Revenue

Step-13: Charitable Solicitation Registration

This is yet another area where it varies between states, but most require it on an annual basis. This mean you need to register with the state before fundraising from any resident of the state. Depending on the scope of your organization you many need to register in other states as well.

As of 13 September 2013, the state of Arizona doesn't require charitable solicitation fundraising registration or renewal. However, some counties and municipalities will still require registration.

Step-14: Business Licenses and Permits

From here you will be all set to start your nonprofit. However, the work isn't over yet. You'll also need to stay in compliance with your nonprofit. Next, consider your required annual filings to remain legal.

Annual Renewal

1. IRS Renewals
    a. IRS Form 990

  b. Due the 15th day of the 5th month following the end of the taxable year.
2. Arizona corporate tax renewals
    a. Filed with the Arizona Department of Revenue by filing Form 99: Exempt Organization Annual Information Return.
    b. Due annually by the 15th day of the 5th month after the end of the fiscal year.
3. Arizona doesn't require sales tax exemption renewal.
4. Arizona requires the filing of an annual report
    a. Filed with the Arizona Corporation Commission - Corporation Division through the Annual Report Form
    b. Can be filed by mail or online.
    c. Costs $10 with expedited processing for $35.
    d. Due annually by the initial registration date.
    e. Nonprofits don't have penalty fees.
    f. Additional information to note:
        i. The report must be filed by an officer listed on the report.
        ii. The annual report can't be used to change the registered agent.
        iii. When filing online print the receipt page for your records.
        iv. When filing by mail be sure to have a cover page.

ARKANSAS

Step-1: Name Your Nonprofit

The name of your nonprofit will establish its brand and will allow you to incorporate with the state. The name you choose cannot conflict with any other organization registered within the state of Arkansas. Make sure the name you choose is available and meets all state requirement. Search through the Arkansas Secretary of State - Business and Commercial Services Division (BCS).

Step-2: Get Initial Directors and Incorporators

The incorporate is the individual who signs the Articles of Incorporation for your business. You will need at least one incorporator, but you can have additional. The directors are the governing body of your nonprofit and are stakeholders in the purpose and success of your nonprofit. You should have at least three directors who are unrelated individuals in order to meet IRS requirements. You'll also want to meet age and residency requirements.

Step-3: Selected a Registered Agent

The registered agent is responsible for receiving legal notices for your nonprofit. A registered agent needs to be physically living in the state and maintain an office open during regular business hours.

Step-4: Articles of Incorporation

The articles of incorporation are the official creation of your nonprofit. They show where and when the nonprofit was formed and provide the necessary information to verify the

nonprofits existence. Make sure your articles of incorporation meet state and IRS requirement.

Form: NPD-1: Articles of Incorporation for Domestic Nonprofit Corporation
Submit To: Arkansas Secretary of State - Business and Commercial Services Division
How to File: Mail or online
Cost: $50 by mail. $45 online.
Time Frame: About 2-4 days

Step-5: Get an Employer Identification Number (EIN)

This is a unique nine-digit number that the IRS assigned to identify your nonprofit. Your EIN is then used to open a bank account, apply for 501(c)(3) status and submit 990 IRS returns.

Form: IRS Form SS-4
Submit To: Internal Revenue Service (IRS)
How to File: Mail, phone, fax or online
Cost: $0
Time Frame: By phone or online is immediate, by fax is 4 days and by mail is 4-5 weeks.

Additional Notes:
- Print EIN before closing session

Step-6: Storing Records

As you start a nonprofit, you will be faced with a number of official documents. Be sure you organize and store all of these records together for easy access later.

Step-7: Initial Governing Policies and Documents

The governing document for your nonprofit is your bylaws since they serve as the operating manual for your organization and need to be consistent with both the law and your articles of incorporation. The first meeting of your Board of Directors should be to review and ratify the bylaws.

You should also create and adopt a conflict of interest policy. This will guide you in what to do if someone in a key position within your nonprofit has competing interests and makes decision that benefit themselves while harming your nonprofit. Organizational interests should be prioritized ahead of personal interests. All conflicts should be disclosed immediately.

Both the bylaws and the conflict of interest policy will need to be approved and adopted before applying to the IRS for 501(c)(3) status.

Step-8: Board of Directors Organizational Meeting

This initial meeting is the most productive and important one. You will approve bylaws, adopt the conflict of interest policy, elect directors, appoint officers and approve any resolutions like opening a bank account. Be sure to record the decisions made in meeting minutes.

Step-9: State Tax Identification Numbers and Accounts

Incorporating a nonprofit means, you will follow all state laws. Requirements vary by state so check with your individual state first.

Arkansas has a consolidated state tax registration application:

Form: Form AR-1R: Combined Business Tax Registration Form
Submit To: Arkansas Department of Finance and Administration

How to File: Mail or in person

Cost: $0. $50 if you are filing a Gross Receipt (Sales Tax) Permit.

Additional Notes:
- Apply 2 weeks before taxable activity starts.
- Don't submit more than 60 days before opening your nonprofit.

Step-10: File for 501(c) Status

This can seem like one of the most difficult steps in starting your nonprofit, but it also offers many benefits. After applying and submitting your documents, the IRS will give you a Determination Letter that officially recognizes your tax-exempt status.

Form: IRS Form 1023, Form 1023-EZ or Form 1024
Submit To: Internal Revenue Service (IRS)
How to File: Mail
Cost: $275 for Form 1023-EZ and $600 for Form 1023
Time Frame: Less than a month for Form 1023-EZ and 3-6 months for Form 1023

Step-11: State Tax Exemption

Once you have your IRS Determination Letter, you next need to figure out your state's requirements for tax-exempt status. This is another area that varies by state. You may also need to do periodic renewals for tax-exempt status.

For state income tax exemption in Arkansas you need to do the following:

Form: Form AR1023CT: Application for Income Tax Exempt Status
Submit To: Arkansas Department of Finance and Administration
Cost: $0

Additional Notes:
- Submit a copy of your IRS Determination Letter to apply.
- Include the first two pages of IRS Form 1023 and a statement declaring exemption under ACA 26-51-303 or ACA 26-51-309.
- If you are submitting without an IRS Determination Letter, you should use Form AR1023CT with a copy of articles of incorporation and a copy of the bylaws.

For state sales tax exemption in Arkansas you need to do the following:

Form: SSTGB Form F0003: Exemption Certificate
Submit To: Arkansas Department of Finance and Administration
Additional Notes:
- In Arkansas, most nonprofits don't get a general exemption; but some charitable sales are exempted under specific conditions.
- The certificate of exemption is used to exempt a nonprofit organization from sales tax in certain purchases.

Step-12: Charitable Solicitation Registration

This is yet another area where it varies between states, but most require it on an annual basis. This mean you need to register with the state before fundraising from any resident of the state. Depending on the scope of your organization you may need to register in other states as well.

Overseen By: Arkansas Secretary of State - Business and Commercial Services Division (BCS)

Exemptions:
1. Less than $25,000 contributions in a calendar year
2. Religious organizations

3. Educational institutions
4. Political organizations and candidates
5. Government organizations
6. Individuals who are soliciting on behalf of an exempt organization
7. Affiliates and chapters

To file in Arkansas, you need to do the following:

Form: Charitable Organization Registration Form (URS) along with Form CR-02: Charitable Organization Consent for Service or Form CR-01: Charitable Organization Registration Form
Submit To: Arkansas Secretary of State - Business and Commercial Services Division
How to File: Mail or email
Cost: $0

Additional Notes:
- Applications must be notarized
- The signature of a officer, director or incorporator is required

Step-13: Business Licenses and Permits

From here you will be all set to start your nonprofit. However, the work isn't over yet. You'll also need to stay in compliance with your nonprofit. Next, consider your required annual filings to remain legal.

Annual Renewal

1. IRS Renewals
    a. IRS Form 990
    b. Due the 15th day of the 5th month following the end of the taxable year.

2. Arkansas has no renewal requirements for corporate income tax exemption.
3. Arkansas doesn't offer general exemptions to sales tax, so there is no renewal.
4. The Arkansas annual report requires the following:
    a. Submit the Annual Report Form to the Arkansas Secretary of State - Business and Commercial Services Division (BCS)
    b. It can be submitted by mail, in person or online
    c. Costs $0
    d. Due annually by August 1st
5. Charitable Solicitation Renewal
    a. Filed with the Arkansas Secretary of State - Business and Commercial Services Division (BCS)
    b. Form URS or Form CR-03: Annual Financial Report Form
    c. Filed by mail or email
    d. Costs $0
    e. Renewal is annually by May 15th for organizations with a fiscal year that ends 12/31 and 6 months after the end of the fiscal year for other end dates.
    f. Submissions must be notarized.
    g. Be sure to attach all necessary documents.

CALIFORNIA

Step-1: Name Your Nonprofit

The name of your nonprofit will establish its brand and will allow you to incorporate with the state. The name you choose cannot conflict with any other organization registered within the state of California. Make sure the name you choose is available and meets all state requirement. Search through the California Secretary of State - Business Programs Division.

Step-2: Choose a Corporation Structure

There are four choices of corporation structures for nonprofits in California:
1. Religious Corporations who are primarily or exclusively for religious purposes.
2. Public Benefit Corporations are those seeking federal and state tax exemptions for charitable purposes, as a civic league or as a social welfare organization.
3. Mutual Benefit Corporations are nonprofits that may or may not see tax exemptions. These corporations can't create the impression of being public, charitable or religious.
4. Mutual Benefit Common Interest Development (CID) Corporations are formed because of the Davis-Stirling Common Interest Development Act for the purpose of managing a common interest development such as a homeowner's association. These can be unincorporated.

Step-3: Get Initial Directors and Incorporators

The incorporate is the individual who signs the Articles of Incorporation for your business. You will need at least one incorporator, but you can have additional. The directors are the governing body of your nonprofit and are stakeholders in the purpose and success of your nonprofit. You should have at least three directors who are unrelated individuals in order to meet IRS requirements. You'll also want to meet age and residency requirements.

Step-4: Selected a Registered Agent

The registered agent is responsible for receiving legal notices for your nonprofit. A registered agent needs to be physically living in the state and maintain an office open during regular business hours.

Step-5: Articles of Incorporation
The articles of incorporation are the official creation of your nonprofit. They show where and when the nonprofit was formed and provide the necessary information to verify the nonprofits existence. Make sure your articles of incorporation meet state and IRS requirement.

Form: There are four templates to choose from depending on your corporation structure:
1. Form ARTS-MU: Articles of Incorporation - Mutual Benefit Corporation
2. Form ARTS-PB-501(c)(3): Articles of Incorporation - Public Benefit Corporation
3. Form ARTS-RE: Articles of Incorporation - Religious Corporation
4. Form ARTS-CID: Articles of Incorporation - Common-Interest Development Corporation

Submit To: California Secretary of State - Business Programs Division
How to File: Mail or in person
Cost: $30 by mail. $45 in person. Optional $250-500 preclearance service. Optional $350-500 expedited fee.
Time Frame: Varies
Step-6: Get an Employer Identification Number (EIN)

This is a unique nine-digit number that the IRS assigned to identify your nonprofit. Your EIN is then used to open a bank account, apply for 501(c)(3) status and submit 990 IRS returns.

Form: IRS Form SS-4
Submit To: Internal Revenue Service (IRS)
How to File: Mail, phone, fax or online
Cost: $0
Time Frame: By phone or online is immediate, by fax is 4 days and by mail is 4-5 weeks.

Additional Notes:
- Print EIN before closing session

Step-7: Storing Records

As you start a nonprofit, you will be faced with a number of official documents. Be sure you organize and store all of these records together for easy access later.

Step-8: Initial Governing Policies and Documents

The governing document for your nonprofit is your bylaws since they serve as the operating manual for your organization and need to be consistent with both the law and your articles of incorporation. The first meeting of your Board of Directors should be to review and ratify the bylaws.

You should also create and adopt a conflict of interest policy. This will guide you in what to do if someone in a key position within your nonprofit has competing interests and makes decision that benefit themselves while harming your nonprofit. Organizational interests should be prioritized ahead of personal interests. All conflicts should be disclosed immediately.

Both the bylaws and the conflict of interest policy will need to be approved and adopted before applying to the IRS for 501(c)(3) status.

Step-9: Board of Directors Organizational Meeting

This initial meeting is the most productive and important one. You will approve bylaws, adopt the conflict of interest policy, elect directors, appoint officers and approve any resolutions like opening a bank account. Be sure to record the decisions made in meeting minutes.

Step-10: State Tax Identification Numbers and Accounts

Incorporating a nonprofit means, you will follow all state laws. Requirements vary by state so check with your individual state first.

If you are going to have employees the state of California requires you to have a California Employer Identification Number. You can apply for this online for free through the State of California - Employment Development Department.

You will also need to get a seller's permit if you are going to collect sales tax on items sold, use a tax account and other permits and licenses. Apply for these through the California State Board of Equalization for free.

Until you apply for and get tax exempt status in the state of California, you may still need to pay franchise and income taxes. The minimum franchise tax is $800. No registration is needed with the Franchise Tax Board, but you may need to pay the minimum tax until you get your exempt status. Contact the State of California - Franchise Tax Board for more information.

Step-11: File for 501(c) Status

This can seem like one of the most difficult steps in starting your nonprofit, but it also offers many benefits. After applying and submitting your documents, the IRS will give you a Determination Letter that officially recognizes your tax-exempt status.

Form: IRS Form 1023, Form 1023-EZ or Form 1024
Submit To: Internal Revenue Service (IRS)
How to File: Mail
Cost: $275 for Form 1023-EZ and $600 for Form 1023
Time Frame: Less than a month for Form 1023-EZ and 3-6 months for Form 1023

Step-12: State Tax Exemption

Once you have your IRS Determination Letter, you next need to figure out your state's requirements for tax-exempt status. This is another area that varies by state. You may also need to do periodic renewals for tax-exempt status.

To obtain state income tax exemption in the state of California, you need to do the following:

Form: Form 3500: Exemption Application or Form 3500A: Submission of Exemption Request
Submit To: California Franchise Tax Board
Cost: $25. $0 for exemption request.
Additional Notes:
- Form 3500A is to be used if you have an IRS Determination Letter and Form 3500 is for if you don't have an IRS Determination Letter.

For state sales tax exemption in California you need to do the following:
Submit To: California State Board of Equalization
Cost: $0

In California, nonprofits can also be exempt from local property taxation called Welfare Exemption. This is only available to qualifying organizations through the Board of Equalization and county assessors' offices.

Step-13: Charitable Solicitation Registration

This is yet another area where it varies between states, but most require it on an annual basis. This mean you need to register with the state before fundraising from any resident of the state. Depending on the scope of your organization you many need to register in other states as well.

Overseen By: California Attorney General - Registry of Charitable Trusts

Exemptions:
1. Educational institutions
2. Religious organizations

To file in California, you need to do the following:

Form: Charitable Organization Registration Form (URS) or Form CT-1: Initial Registration Form
Submit To: California Attorney General - Registry of Charitable Trusts
How to File: Mail
Cost: $25

Additional Notes:
- Must register within 30 days of receiving assets that are held in trust.
- Attach all appropriate documents.
- Maybe signed by an authorized individual or director.
- Signatures must be notarized.

Step-14: Business Licenses and Permits

From here you will be all set to start your nonprofit. However, the work isn't over yet. You'll also need to stay in compliance with your nonprofit. Next, consider your required annual filings to remain legal.

Annual Renewal

1. IRS Renewals
    a. IRS Form 990
    b. Due the 15th day of the 5th month following the end of the taxable year.
2. California Corporate Tax Exemption Renewal
    a. Filed with the California Franchise Tax Board
    b. File one or more of the following forms:
        i. Form 199: California Exempt Organization Annual Information Return
        ii. FTB 199N: Annual Electronic Filing Requirement for Small Exempt Organizations
        iii. Form 109: California Exempt Organization Business Income Tax Return
        iv. Form 100: California Corporation Franchise or Income Tax Return
    c. Due four and a half months after the end of the fiscal year.
3. California does not have sales tax exemption renewal. California doesn't offer general exemptions to nonprofits.
4. California requires a statement of information.
    a. Form SI-100: Statement of Information - Nonprofit
    b. Filed with the California Secretary of State - Business Programs Division
    c. Filed by mail, in person or online.
    d. Costs $20 or $25 for agricultural cooperative corporations.
    e. Online version is processed in about 1 day.

- f. Due biennially at the end of the month when the Articles of Incorporation were first filed. Can be submitted up to 5 months early.
- g. Late penalty of $50.
5. Charitable Solicitation Renewal
    - a. Filed with the California Attorney General - Registry of Charitable Trusts
    - b. Form RRF-1: Annual Registration Renewal Report
    - c. Filed by mail
    - d. Costs $0-300 depending on your gross annual revenue.
    - e. Renewal is annually four and a half months after close of your fiscal year.
    - f. Attach all required documents.
    - g. Any authorized individual or director may sign.
    - h. No notary is required.

COLORADO

Step-1: Name Your Nonprofit

The name of your nonprofit will establish its brand and will allow you to incorporate with the state. The name you choose cannot conflict with any other organization registered within the state of Colorado. Make sure the name you choose is available and meets all state requirement. Search through the Colorado Secretary of State.

Step-2: Get Initial Directors and Incorporators

The incorporate is the individual who signs the Articles of Incorporation for your business. You will need at least one incorporator, but you can have additional. The directors are the governing body of your nonprofit and are stakeholders in the purpose and success of your nonprofit. You should have at least three directors who are unrelated individuals in order to meet IRS requirements. You'll also want to meet age and residency requirements.

Step-3: Selected a Registered Agent

The registered agent is responsible for receiving legal notices for your nonprofit. A registered agent needs to be physically living in the state and maintain an office open during regular business hours.

Step-4: Articles of Incorporation

The articles of incorporation are the official creation of your nonprofit. They show where and when the nonprofit was formed and provide the necessary information to verify the nonprofits existence. Make sure your articles of incorporation meet state and IRS requirement.

Form: Articles of Incorporation for a Nonprofit Corporation
Submit To: Colorado Secretary of State
How to File: Online
Cost: $50
Time Frame: Immediate

Step-5: Get an Employer Identification Number (EIN)

This is a unique nine-digit number that the IRS assigned to identify your nonprofit. Your EIN is then used to open a bank account, apply for 501(c)(3) status and submit 990 IRS returns.

Form: IRS Form SS-4
Submit To: Internal Revenue Service (IRS)
How to File: Mail, phone, fax or online
Cost: $0
Time Frame: By phone or online is immediate, by fax is 4 days and by mail is 4-5 weeks.

Additional Notes:
- Print EIN before closing session

Step-6: Storing Records

As you start a nonprofit, you will be faced with a number of official documents. Be sure you organize and store all of these records together for easy access later.

Step-7: Initial Governing Policies and Documents

The governing document for your nonprofit is your bylaws since they serve as the operating manual for your organization and need to be consistent with both the law and

your articles of incorporation. The first meeting of your Board of Directors should be to review and ratify the bylaws.

You should also create and adopt a conflict of interest policy. This will guide you in what to do if someone in a key position within your nonprofit has competing interests and makes decision that benefit themselves while harming your nonprofit. Organizational interests should be prioritized ahead of personal interests. All conflicts should be disclosed immediately.

Both the bylaws and the conflict of interest policy will need to be approved and adopted before applying to the IRS for 501(c)(3) status.

Step-8: Board of Directors Organizational Meeting

This initial meeting is the most productive and important one. You will approve bylaws, adopt the conflict of interest policy, elect directors, appoint officers and approve any resolutions like opening a bank account. Be sure to record the decisions made in meeting minutes.

Step-9: State Tax Identification Numbers and Accounts

Incorporating a nonprofit means, you will follow all state laws. Requirements vary by state so check with your individual state first.

Colorado has a consolidated state tax registration application online, or you can submit two registrations by mail.

For a sales tax account and/or wage withholding account:

Form: Form CR-0100: Colorado Sales Tax Withholding Account Application
Submit To: Colorado Department of Revenue

How to File: Mail, in person or online

Cost: $8 for a charitable license. $50 deposit for a retail sales tax license.

Time Frame: About 2-3 weeks online. About 4-6 weeks by mail. Immediate in person.

If you are going to hire employees and withhold income, then you'll need to get an unemployment insurance tax account number and rate:

Form: Form UITL-100: Application for Unemployment Insurance Account and Determination of Employer Liability

Submit To: Colorado Department of Labor and Employment

How to File: Mail or online

Cost: $0

Step-10: File for 501(c) Status

This can seem like one of the most difficult steps in starting your nonprofit, but it also offers many benefits. After applying and submitting your documents, the IRS will give you a Determination Letter that officially recognizes your tax-exempt status.

Form: IRS Form 1023, Form 1023-EZ or Form 1024

Submit To: Internal Revenue Service (IRS)

How to File: Mail

Cost: $275 for Form 1023-EZ and $600 for Form 1023

Time Frame: Less than a month for Form 1023-EZ and 3-6 months for Form 1023

Step-11: State Tax Exemption

Once you have your IRS Determination Letter, you next need to figure out your state's requirements for tax-exempt status. This is another area that varies by state. You may also need to do periodic renewals for tax-exempt status.

In Colorado, you obtain your state income tax exemption when you get your IRS Determination Letter.

For sales tax and state-administered local tax exemption in Colorado you need to do the following:

Form: DR 0715: Application for Sales Tax Exemption and DR 0716: Statement of Nonprofit - Church, Synagogue or Organization
Submit To: Colorado Department of Revenue
Cost: $0

Additional Notes:
- When approved you will get a Certificate of Exemption

Step-12: Charitable Solicitation Registration

This is yet another area where it varies between states, but most require it on an annual basis. This mean you need to register with the state before fundraising from any resident of the state. Depending on the scope of your organization you may need to register in other states as well.

Overseen By: Colorado Secretary of State

Exemptions:
1. Less than $25,000 gross revenue per fiscal year
2. Religious organizations
3. Less than 10 donors nationwide per fiscal year
4. Political organizations
5. Appeals for individuals

To file in Colorado, you need to do the following:

Form: Charitable Organization Registration Form (URS)
Submit To: Colorado Secretary of State
How to File: Online
Cost: $10

Additional Notes:
- Disclose contracts with paid solicitors.
- Must be signed electronically by an authorized officer.
- After approval, you are given a registration number and printable certificate of registration.

Step-13: Business Licenses and Permits

From here you will be all set to start your nonprofit. However, the work isn't over yet. You'll also need to stay in compliance with your nonprofit. Next, consider your required annual filings to remain legal.

Annual Renewal

1. IRS Renewals
    a. IRS Form 990
    b. Due the 15th day of the 5th month following the end of the taxable year.
2. Colorado has no renewal requirements for corporate income tax exemption.
3. Colorado doesn't have a renewal requirement for sales tax exemption.
4. Colorado requires a periodic report
    a. Filed with the Colorado Secretary of State
    b. Filed online
    c. Costs $10

- d. Due annually during the 3 month period beginning with the first day of the anniversary month of formation.
- e. Can be filed 2 months early.
- f. Must be filed online and paid with by credit/debit card.
- g. May be filed by anyone with authority.

5. Charitable Solicitation Renewal
    - a. Filed with the Colorado Secretary of State
    - b. Filed by online
    - c. Costs $10
    - d. Renewal is annually four and a half months after the close of the fiscal year
    - e. Colorado automatically offers a 3 month extension on the deadline
    - f. Must be signed electronically by an authorized officer
    - g. File with your annual financial report

CONNECTICUT

Step-1: Name Your Nonprofit

The name of your nonprofit will establish its brand and will allow you to incorporate with the state. The name you choose cannot conflict with any other organization registered within the state of Connecticut. Make sure the name you choose is available and meets all state requirement. Search through the Connecticut Secretary of State - Commercial Recording Division.

Step-2: Get Initial Directors and Incorporators

The incorporate is the individual who signs the Articles of Incorporation for your business. You will need at least one incorporator, but you can have additional. The directors are the governing body of your nonprofit and are stakeholders in the purpose and success of your nonprofit. You should have at least three directors who are unrelated individuals in order to meet IRS requirements. You'll also want to meet age and residency requirements.

Step-3: Selected a Registered Agent

The registered agent is responsible for receiving legal notices for your nonprofit. A registered agent needs to be physically living in the state and maintain an office open during regular business hours.

Step-4: Articles of Incorporation

The articles of incorporation are the official creation of your nonprofit. They show where and when the nonprofit was formed and provide the necessary information to verify the

nonprofits existence. Make sure your articles of incorporation meet state and IRS requirement.

Form: Certificate of Incorporation
Submit To: Connecticut Secretary of State - Commercial Recording Division
How to File: Mail or fax
Cost: $50 + optional $50 expedite
Time Frame: About 3-5 days. About 24 hours expedited.

Step-5: Get an Employer Identification Number (EIN)

This is a unique nine-digit number that the IRS assigned to identify your nonprofit. Your EIN is then used to open a bank account, apply for 501(c)(3) status and submit 990 IRS returns.

Form: IRS Form SS-4
Submit To: Internal Revenue Service (IRS)
How to File: Mail, phone, fax or online
Cost: $0
Time Frame: By phone or online is immediate, by fax is 4 days and by mail is 4-5 weeks.

Additional Notes:
- Print EIN before closing session

Step-6: Storing Records

As you start a nonprofit, you will be faced with a number of official documents. Be sure you organize and store all of these records together for easy access later.

Step-7: Initial Governing Policies and Documents

The governing document for your nonprofit is your bylaws since they serve as the operating manual for your organization and need to be consistent with both the law and your articles of incorporation. The first meeting of your Board of Directors should be to review and ratify the bylaws.

You should also create and adopt a conflict of interest policy. This will guide you in what to do if someone in a key position within your nonprofit has competing interests and makes decision that benefit themselves while harming your nonprofit. Organizational interests should be prioritized ahead of personal interests. All conflicts should be disclosed immediately.

Both the bylaws and the conflict of interest policy will need to be approved and adopted before applying to the IRS for 501(c)(3) status.

Step-8: Board of Directors Organizational Meeting

This initial meeting is the most productive and important one. You will approve bylaws, adopt the conflict of interest policy, elect directors, appoint officers and approve any resolutions like opening a bank account. Be sure to record the decisions made in meeting minutes.

Step-9: State Tax Identification Numbers and Accounts

Incorporating a nonprofit means, you will follow all state laws. Requirements vary by state so check with your individual state first.

Connecticut has a consolidated state tax registration application. You get a Connecticut Tax Registration Number and then apply for exemption that includes corporation business tax, business entity tax, sales and use taxes, income tax withholding and motor vehicles fuel tax:

Form: REG-1: Business Tax Registration Application
Submit To: State of Connecticut - Department of Revenue Services
How to File: Mail, in person or online
Cost: $100 for state sales tax license
Time Frame: About 15-20 days online. About 2-3 weeks by mail. Immediate in person.

Step-10: File for 501(c) Status

This can seem like one of the most difficult steps in starting your nonprofit, but it also offers many benefits. After applying and submitting your documents, the IRS will give you a Determination Letter that officially recognizes your tax-exempt status.

Form: IRS Form 1023, Form 1023-EZ or Form 1024
Submit To: Internal Revenue Service (IRS)
How to File: Mail
Cost: $275 for Form 1023-EZ and $600 for Form 1023
Time Frame: Less than a month for Form 1023-EZ and 3-6 months for Form 1023

Step-11: State Tax Exemption

Once you have your IRS Determination Letter, you next need to figure out your state's requirements for tax-exempt status. This is another area that varies by state. You may also need to do periodic renewals for tax-exempt status.

In Connecticut to get your state tax exemption, you need to submit a copy of your IRS Determination Letter with your REG-1 Application to the Connecticut Department of Revenue Services.
In Connecticut, you are automatically exempt from sales tax when you get your IRS Determination Letter.

Step-12: Charitable Solicitation Registration

This is yet another area where it varies between states, but most require it on an annual basis. This mean you need to register with the state before fundraising from any resident of the state. Depending on the scope of your organization you many need to register in other states as well.

Overseen By: Connecticut Department of Consumer Protection

Exemptions:
1. Less than $50,000 annual contributions with no paid solicitors
2. Religious organizations
3. PTAs
4. Exempt organization appeals

To file in Connecticut, you need to do the following:

Form: Charitable Organization Registration Form (URS) or Initial Charitable Organization Registration Application
Submit To: Connecticut Department of Consumer Protection
How to File: Mail or online
Cost: $50

Additional Notes:
- Include all required documents
- Must be signed by two authorized representatives
- Does not need to be notarized
- Exemption must be submitted by email

Step-13: Business Licenses and Permits

From here you will be all set to start your nonprofit. However, the work isn't over yet. You'll also need to stay in compliance with your nonprofit. Next, consider your required annual filings to remain legal.

Annual Renewal

1. IRS Renewals
    a. IRS Form 990
    b. Due the 15th day of the 5th month following the end of the taxable year.
2. Connecticut has no renewal requirements for corporate income tax exemption.
3. Connecticut has no renewal requirements for sales tax exemption.
4. Connecticut requires an annual report
    a. Filed with the Connecticut Secretary of State - Commercial Recording Division
    b. Must be filed online
    c. Costs $50
    d. Due annually at the end of the month when the corporation was first registered
    e. Annual reports are not needed for religious organizations and statutory trusts
    f. May be filed by anyone with authority
5. Charitable Solicitation Renewal
    a. Filed with the Connecticut Department of Consumer Protection
    b. Form Charitable Organization Renewal Notice
    c. Filed by mail or online
    d. Costs $50
    e. Due 11 months after the fiscal year ends
    f. Attach IRS Form 990

DELAWARE

Step-1: Name Your Nonprofit

The name of your nonprofit will establish its brand and will allow you to incorporate with the state. The name you choose cannot conflict with any other organization registered within the state of Delaware. Make sure the name you choose is available and meets all state requirement. Search through the Delaware Department of State - Division of Corporations.

Step-2: Choose a Nonprofit Structure

Delaware offers the option to form two types of nonprofit corporations: exempt and non-stock. Exempt corporations aren't subject to annual franchise tax in Delaware. In order to qualify for exemption, the organization needs to meet the requirements of 501(b). You will likely qualify if your nonprofit meets one of the following:
1. Exempt under IRS Code 501(c)(3) or a similar section
2. Is a civic organization
3. Is a charitable or fraternal organization
4. Is listed in 8106(a) Title 9
5. Is organized for primary charitable or religious purposes
6. Is organized not for profit and has no part of net earnings benefiting any member or individual

If your corporation doesn't meet the qualifications for exemption, then you'll need to file as a non-stock non-profit corporation.

Step-3: Get Initial Directors and Incorporators

The incorporate is the individual who signs the Articles of Incorporation for your business. You will need at least one incorporator, but you can have additional. The directors are the governing body of your nonprofit and are stakeholders in the purpose and success of your nonprofit. You should have at least three directors who are unrelated individuals in order to meet IRS requirements. You'll also want to meet age and residency requirements.

Step-4: Selected a Registered Agent

The registered agent is responsible for receiving legal notices for your nonprofit. A registered agent needs to be physically living in the state and maintain an office open during regular business hours.

Step-5: Articles of Incorporation

The articles of incorporation are the official creation of your nonprofit. They show where and when the nonprofit was formed and provide the necessary information to verify the nonprofits existence. Make sure your articles of incorporation meet state and IRS requirement.

Form: Certificate of Incorporation for Exempt Corporation
Submit To: Delaware Department of State - Division of Corporations
How to File: Mail or fax
Cost: $89 + $9 for extra pages. Option $50-1000 expedite.
Time Frame: About 3 weeks. About 24 hours with a $50 expedite. Same day for $100 expedite. About two hours for $500 expedite. One hour for $1000 expedite.

Additional Notes:
- Be sure to include a cover letter

Step-6: Get an Employer Identification Number (EIN)

This is a unique nine-digit number that the IRS assigned to identify your nonprofit. Your EIN is then used to open a bank account, apply for 501(c)(3) status and submit 990 IRS returns.

Form: IRS Form SS-4
Submit To: Internal Revenue Service (IRS)
How to File: Mail, phone, fax or online
Cost: $0
Time Frame: By phone or online is immediate, by fax is 4 days and by mail is 4-5 weeks

Additional Notes:
- Print EIN before closing session

Step-7: Storing Records

As you start a nonprofit, you will be faced with a number of official documents. Be sure you organize and store all of these records together for easy access later.

Step-8: Initial Governing Policies and Documents

The governing document for your nonprofit is your bylaws since they serve as the operating manual for your organization and need to be consistent with both the law and your articles of incorporation. The first meeting of your Board of Directors should be to review and ratify the bylaws.

You should also create and adopt a conflict of interest policy. This will guide you in what to do if someone in a key position within your nonprofit has competing interests and makes decision that benefit themselves while harming your nonprofit. Organizational interests should be prioritized ahead of personal interests. All conflicts should be disclosed immediately.

Both the bylaws and the conflict of interest policy will need to be approved and adopted before applying to the IRS for 501(c)(3) status.

Step-9: Board of Directors Organizational Meeting

This initial meeting is the most productive and important one. You will approve bylaws, adopt the conflict of interest policy, elect directors, appoint officers and approve any resolutions like opening a bank account. Be sure to record the decisions made in meeting minutes.

Delaware requires two days written notice to attendees.

Step-10: State Tax Identification Numbers and Accounts

Incorporating a nonprofit means, you will follow all state laws. Requirements vary by state so check with your individual state first.

Delaware nonprofit corporations don't have to obtain a business license and don't have to pay the accompanying gross receipts tax on the sales of services or goods; however, they do need to register with the Division of Revenue.

Delaware has a consolidated state tax registration application:

Form: CRA: Combined Registration Application for State of Delaware Business License and/or Withholding Agent
Submit To: Delaware Division of Revenue
How to File: Mail or online

Cost: Varies based on accounts/licenses
Time Frame: Varies

Step-11: File for 501(c) Status

This can seem like one of the most difficult steps in starting your nonprofit, but it also offers many benefits. After applying and submitting your documents, the IRS will give you a Determination Letter that officially recognizes your tax-exempt status.

Form: IRS Form 1023, Form 1023-EZ or Form 1024
Submit To: Internal Revenue Service (IRS)
How to File: Mail
Cost: $275 for Form 1023-EZ and $600 for Form 1023
Time Frame: Less than a month for Form 1023-EZ and 3-6 months for Form 1023

Step-12: State Tax Exemption

Once you have your IRS Determination Letter, you next need to figure out your state's requirements for tax-exempt status. This is another area that varies by state. You may also need to do periodic renewals for tax-exempt status.

In Delaware, you obtain your state income tax exemption when you get your IRS Determination Letter.

Delaware does not collect sales tax. Although nonprofits still need to register with the Division of Revenue.

Step-13: Charitable Solicitation Registration
This is yet another area where it varies between states, but most require it on an annual basis. This mean you need to register with the state before fundraising from any resident

of the state. Depending on the scope of your organization you may need to register in other states as well.

Solicitation law in Delaware does not require nonprofits to register with the state. However, disclosures are required during the solicitation process. Some counties and municipalities may require registration.

Step-14: Business Licenses and Permits

From here you will be all set to start your nonprofit. However, the work isn't over yet. You'll also need to stay in compliance with your nonprofit. Next, consider your required annual filings to remain legal.

Annual Renewal

1. IRS Renewals
    a. IRS Form 990
    b. Due the 15th day of the 5th month following the end of the taxable year.
2. Delaware has no renewal requirements for corporate income tax exemption.
3. Delaware doesn't have a state-level sales tax.
4. Delaware requires an annual report
    a. Filed with the Delaware Department of State - Division of Corporations
    b. Must be filed online
    c. Costs $25
    d. Due annually by March 1st
    e. First report is due in the calendar year after initial registration
    f. $125 late fee

DISTRICT OF COLUMBIA

Step-1: Name Your Nonprofit

The name of your nonprofit will establish its brand and will allow you to incorporate with the state. The name you choose cannot conflict with any other organization registered within the District of Columbia. Make sure the name you choose is available and meets all state requirement. Search through the DCRA Corporations Division.

Step-2: Get Initial Directors and Incorporators

The incorporate is the individual who signs the Articles of Incorporation for your business. You will need at least one incorporator, but you can have additional. The directors are the governing body of your nonprofit and are stakeholders in the purpose and success of your nonprofit. You should have at least three directors who are unrelated individuals in order to meet IRS requirements. You'll also want to meet age and residency requirements.

Step-3: Selected a Registered Agent

The registered agent is responsible for receiving legal notices for your nonprofit. A registered agent needs to be physically living in the state and maintain an office open during regular business hours.

Step-4: Articles of Incorporation

The articles of incorporation are the official creation of your nonprofit. They show where and when the nonprofit was formed and provide the necessary information to verify the nonprofits existence. Make sure your articles of incorporation meet state and IRS requirement.

Form: Articles of Incorporation of Domestic Nonprofit Corporation DNP-1
Submit To: DCRA Corporations Division
How to File: Mail, in person or online. Filing in person requires an expedite fee.
Cost: $80. Optional $50-100 expedite.
Time Frame: About 15 days. About 3 days for $50 expedite. Same day for $100 expedite.

Additional Notes:
- If filing online print the last confirmation page to keep for your records.
- For expedited orders include Form EX-1: Expedited Action Form.

Step-5: Get an Employer Identification Number (EIN)

This is a unique nine-digit number that the IRS assigned to identify your nonprofit. Your EIN is then used to open a bank account, apply for 501(c)(3) status and submit 990 IRS returns.

Form: IRS Form SS-4
Submit To: Internal Revenue Service (IRS)
How to File: Mail, phone, fax or online
Cost: $0
Time Frame: By phone or online is immediate, by fax is 4 days and by mail is 4-5 weeks.

Additional Notes:
- Print EIN before closing session

Step-6: Storing Records

As you start a nonprofit, you will be faced with a number of official documents. Be sure you organize and store all of these records together for easy access later.

Step-7: Initial Governing Policies and Documents

The governing document for your nonprofit is your bylaws since they serve as the operating manual for your organization and need to be consistent with both the law and your articles of incorporation. The first meeting of your Board of Directors should be to review and ratify the bylaws.

You should also create and adopt a conflict of interest policy. This will guide you in what to do if someone in a key position within your nonprofit has competing interests and makes decision that benefit themselves while harming your nonprofit. Organizational interests should be prioritized ahead of personal interests. All conflicts should be disclosed immediately.

Both the bylaws and the conflict of interest policy will need to be approved and adopted before applying to the IRS for 501(c)(3) status.

Step-8: Board of Directors Organizational Meeting

This initial meeting is the most productive and important one. You will approve bylaws, adopt the conflict of interest policy, elect directors, appoint officers and approve any resolutions like opening a bank account. Be sure to record the decisions made in meeting minutes.

Step-9: State Tax Identification Numbers and Accounts

Incorporating a nonprofit means, you will follow all state laws. Requirements vary by state so check with your individual state first.

District of Columbia requires the following for tax account registration:

Form: FR 500: D.C. Tax Registration
Submit To: District of Columbia Office of Tax and Revenue
How to File: Online
Cost: $0

Step-10: File for 501(c) Status

This can seem like one of the most difficult steps in starting your nonprofit, but it also offers many benefits. After applying and submitting your documents, the IRS will give you a Determination Letter that officially recognizes your tax-exempt status.

Form: IRS Form 1023, Form 1023-EZ or Form 1024
Submit To: Internal Revenue Service (IRS)
How to File: Mail
Cost: $275 for Form 1023-EZ and $600 for Form 1023
Time Frame: Less than a month for Form 1023-EZ and 3-6 months for Form 1023

Step-11: State Tax Exemption

Once you have your IRS Determination Letter, you next need to figure out your state's requirements for tax-exempt status. This is another area that varies by state. You may also need to do periodic renewals for tax-exempt status.

For income tax exemption and sales tax exemption in the District of Columbia, you need to file online with the D.C. Office of Tax and Revenue for free.

Step-12: Charitable Solicitation Registration

This is yet another area where it varies between states, but most require it on an annual basis. This mean you need to register with the state before fundraising from any resident of the state. Depending on the scope of your organization you may need to register in other states as well.

Overseen By: District of Columbia, Department of Consumer and Regulatory Affairs

Exemptions:
1. Less than $1,500 gross revenue per calendar year and solicitations done by volunteers only
2. Religious organizations
3. Educational institutions
4. Membership organizations

To file, you need to do the following:

Form: Charitable Organization Registration Form (URS) and Basic Business License (BBL-EZ) with two options:
1. D.C. Basic Business License for the Charitable Solicitation Category for $412.50
2. D.C. Basic Business License in the General Category for $324.50

Submit To: District of Columbia, Department of Consumer and Regulatory Affairs
How to File: Online
Cost: $412.50 or $324.50
Additional Notes:
- Attach all necessary documents including:
    - Clean hands self-certification
    - Tax number / certificate
    - Certificate of occupancy
    - Formation documents
    - Bylaws
    - IRS Determination Letter
    - Certified resolution

- o Solicitor information cards
- Notarized signatures aren't required

Step-13: Business Licenses and Permits

From here you will be all set to start your nonprofit. However, the work isn't over yet. You'll also need to stay in compliance with your nonprofit. Next, consider your required annual filings to remain legal.

Annual Renewal

1. IRS Renewals
   a. IRS Form 990
   b. Due the 15th day of the 5th month following the end of the taxable year.
2. District of Columbia has no renewal requirements for corporate income tax exemption.
3. District of Columbia has no ongoing need to renew tax exemption.
4. District of Columbia requires the filing of a two-year report
   a. File with DCRA Corporations Division
   b. Form BRA-25: Two-Year Report for Domestic and Foreign Filing Entity
   c. File by mail, in person or online
   d. Costs $80
   e. Online filing is processed in about 15 days
   f. First report is due by April 1st in the calendar year after registration
   g. Other reports are due by April 1st biennially
   h. $50 late fee
   i. In person, filing requires an additional $100 fee
5. Charitable Solicitation Renewal
   a. Filed with the District of Columbia, Department of Consumer and Regulatory Affairs

b. Form Basic Business License

c. Filed by mail, in person or online

d. Costs $412.50

e. Due biennially at the end of the month prior to your registration month

FLORIDA

Step-1: Name Your Nonprofit

The name of your nonprofit will establish its brand and will allow you to incorporate with the state. The name you choose cannot conflict with any other organization registered within the state of Florida. Make sure the name you choose is available and meets all state requirement. Search through the Florida Department of State - Division of Corporations.

Step-2: Get Initial Directors and Incorporators

The incorporate is the individual who signs the Articles of Incorporation for your business. You will need at least one incorporator, but you can have additional. The directors are the governing body of your nonprofit and are stakeholders in the purpose and success of your nonprofit. You should have at least three directors who are unrelated individuals in order to meet IRS requirements. You'll also want to meet age and residency requirements.

Step-3: Selected a Registered Agent

The registered agent is responsible for receiving legal notices for your nonprofit. A registered agent needs to be physically living in the state and maintain an office open during regular business hours.

Step-4: Articles of Incorporation

The articles of incorporation are the official creation of your nonprofit. They show where and when the nonprofit was formed and provide the necessary information to verify the

nonprofits existence. Make sure your articles of incorporation meet state and IRS requirement.

Form: Non-Profit Articles of Incorporation
Submit To: Florida Department of State - Division of Corporations
How to File: Mail or online
Cost: $35 filing fee + $35 designation of registered agent fee for a total $70 state fee
Time Frame: About 1-3 days online. About 8-17 days by mail.

Additional Notes:
- Provide a state-prescribed cover letter, an original and a copy of the articles of incorporation.

Step-5: Get an Employer Identification Number (EIN)

This is a unique nine-digit number that the IRS assigned to identify your nonprofit. Your EIN is then used to open a bank account, apply for 501(c)(3) status and submit 990 IRS returns.

Form: IRS Form SS-4
Submit To: Internal Revenue Service (IRS)
How to File: Mail, phone, fax or online
Cost: $0
Time Frame: By phone or online is immediate, by fax is 4 days and by mail is 4-5 weeks

Additional Notes:
- Print EIN before closing session

Step-6: Storing Records

As you start a nonprofit, you will be faced with a number of official documents. Be sure you organize and store all of these records together for easy access later.

Step-7: Initial Governing Policies and Documents

The governing document for your nonprofit is your bylaws since they serve as the operating manual for your organization and need to be consistent with both the law and your articles of incorporation. The first meeting of your Board of Directors should be to review and ratify the bylaws.

You should also create and adopt a conflict of interest policy. This will guide you in what to do if someone in a key position within your nonprofit has competing interests and makes decision that benefit themselves while harming your nonprofit. Organizational interests should be prioritized ahead of personal interests. All conflicts should be disclosed immediately.

Both the bylaws and the conflict of interest policy will need to be approved and adopted before applying to the IRS for 501(c)(3) status.

Step-8: Board of Directors Organizational Meeting

This initial meeting is the most productive and important one. You will approve bylaws, adopt the conflict of interest policy, elect directors, appoint officers and approve any resolutions like opening a bank account. Be sure to record the decisions made in meeting minutes.

Step-9: State Tax Identification Numbers and Accounts

Incorporating a nonprofit means, you will follow all state laws. Requirements vary by state so check with your individual state first.

Florida has a consolidated state tax registration application:

Form: DR-1: Florida Business Tax Application
Submit To: Florida Department of Revenue
How to File: Mail or online
Cost: $0 + $5 sales tax registration

Step-10: File for 501(c) Status

This can seem like one of the most difficult steps in starting your nonprofit, but it also offers many benefits. After applying and submitting your documents, the IRS will give you a Determination Letter that officially recognizes your tax-exempt status.

Form: IRS Form 1023, Form 1023-EZ or Form 1024
Submit To: Internal Revenue Service (IRS)
How to File: Mail
Cost: $275 for Form 1023-EZ and $600 for Form 1023
Time Frame: Less than a month for Form 1023-EZ and 3-6 months for Form 1023

Step-11: State Tax Exemption

Once you have your IRS Determination Letter, you next need to figure out your state's requirements for tax exempt status. This is another area that varies by state. You may also need to do periodic renewals for tax exempt status.

For state income tax exemption in Florida contact the Florida Department of Revenue.

For state sales tax exemption in Florida you need to do the following:
Form: DR-5: Application for a Consumer's Certificate of Exemption
Submit To: Florida Department of Revenue

Cost: $0

Step-12: Charitable Solicitation Registration

This is yet another area where it varies between states, but most require it on an annual basis. This means you need to register with the state before fundraising from any resident of the state. Depending on the scope of your organization you may need to register in other states as well.

Overseen By: Florida Department of Agriculture and Consumer Services - Division of Consumer Services.

Exemptions:
1. Less than $25,000 total revenue during the preceding fiscal year
2. Religious organizations
3. Educational institutions
4. Membership organizations
5. Political groups
6. Appeals for individuals

To file, you need to do the following:

Form: Charitable Organizations / Sponsors Registration Application
Submit To: Florida Department of Agriculture and Consumer Services - Division of Consumer Services
How to File: Mail or online
Cost: $10-400, depending on contributions the previous fiscal year

Additional Notes:
- Attach all necessary documents

- CFO or treasurer notarized signature required

Step-13: Business Licenses and Permits

From here you will be all set to start your nonprofit. However, the work isn't over yet. You'll also need to stay in compliance with your nonprofit. Next, consider your required annual filings to remain legal.

Annual Renewal

1. IRS Renewals
    a. IRS Form 990
    b. Due the 15th day of the 5th month following the end of the taxable year.
2. Florida has no renewal requirements for corporate income tax exemption.
3. Florida Sales Tax Exemption Renewal
    a. Filed with the Florida Department of Revenue
    b. Due every 5 years from the date of issue
4. Florida requires an annual report
    a. Filed with the Florida Department of State - Division of Corporations
    b. Filed online
    c. Costs $61.25
    d. Due annually by May 1st
5. Charitable Solicitation Renewal
    a. Filed with the Florida Department of Agriculture and Consumer Services - Division of Consumer Services
    b. You will be mailed a renewal form
    c. Filed by mail or online
    d. Costs $10-400 depending on contributions in the previous fiscal year
    e. Renewed annually between initial registration day and 60 days prior
    f. Include all needed attachments including a financial report

GEORGIA

Step-1: Name Your Nonprofit

The name of your nonprofit will establish its brand and will allow you to incorporate with the state. The name you choose cannot conflict with any other organization registered within the state of Georgia. Make sure the name you choose is available and meets all state requirement. Search through the Georgia Secretary of State.

Step-2: Get Initial Directors and Incorporators

The incorporate is the individual who signs the Articles of Incorporation for your business. You will need at least one incorporator, but you can have additional. The directors are the governing body of your nonprofit and are stakeholders in the purpose and success of your nonprofit. You should have at least three directors who are unrelated individuals in order to meet IRS requirements. You'll also want to meet age and residency requirements.

Step-3: Selected a Registered Agent

The registered agent is responsible for receiving legal notices for your nonprofit. A registered agent needs to be physically living in the state and maintain an office open during regular business hours.

Step-4: Articles of Incorporation

The articles of incorporation are the official creation of your nonprofit. They show where and when the nonprofit was formed and provide the necessary information to verify the nonprofits existence. Make sure your articles of incorporation meet state and IRS requirement.

Form: Transmittal Information from Georgia Profit or Nonprofit Corporation
Submit To: Georgia Secretary of State
How to File: Mail or online
Cost: $100
Time Frame: About 5-12 days

Step-5: Publish Your Incorporation

New nonprofit corporations in Georgia are required to publish a notice of incorporation no later than the day after filing.

Step-6: Get an Employer Identification Number (EIN)

This is a unique nine-digit number that the IRS assigned to identify your nonprofit. Your EIN is then used to open a bank account, apply for 501(c)(3) status and submit 990 IRS returns.

Form: IRS Form SS-4
Submit To: Internal Revenue Service (IRS)
How to File: Mail, phone, fax or online
Cost: $0
Time Frame: By phone or online is immediate, by fax is 4 days and by mail is 4-5 weeks.

Additional Notes:
- Print EIN before the closing session

Step-7: Storing Records

As you start a nonprofit, you will be faced with a number of official documents. Be sure you organize and store all of these records together for easy access later.

Step-8: Initial Governing Policies and Documents

The governing document for your nonprofit is your bylaws since they serve as the operating manual for your organization and need to be consistent with both the law and your articles of incorporation. The first meeting of your Board of Directors should be to review and ratify the bylaws.

You should also create and adopt a conflict of interest policy. This will guide you in what to do if someone in a key position within your nonprofit has competing interests and makes a decision that benefits themselves while harming your nonprofit. Organizational interests should be prioritized ahead of personal interests. All conflicts should be disclosed immediately.

Both the bylaws and the conflict of interest policy will need to be approved and adopted before applying to the IRS for 501(c)(3) status.

Step-9: Board of Directors Organizational Meeting

This initial meeting is the most productive and important one. You will approve bylaws, adopt the conflict of interest policy, elect directors, appoint officers and approve any resolutions like opening a bank account. Be sure to record the decisions made in meeting minutes.

Step-10: State Tax Identification Numbers and Accounts

Incorporating a nonprofit means, you will follow all state laws. Requirements vary by state so check with your individual state first.
Georgia has a consolidated state tax registration application. File with the Georgia Department of Revenue online for free.

Step-11: File for 501(c) Status

This can seem like one of the most difficult steps in starting your nonprofit, but it also offers many benefits. After applying and submitting your documents, the IRS will give you a Determination Letter that officially recognizes your tax-exempt status.

Form: IRS Form 1023, Form 1023-EZ or Form 1024
Submit To: Internal Revenue Service (IRS)
How to File: Mail
Cost: $275 for Form 1023-EZ and $600 for Form 1023
Time Frame: Less than a month for Form 1023-EZ and 3-6 months for Form 1023

Step-12: State Tax Exemption

Once you have your IRS Determination Letter, you next need to figure out your state's requirements for tax-exempt status. This is another area that varies by state. You may also need to do periodic renewals for tax-exempt status.

For both state income tax and state sales tax exemption, you can file with the Georgia Department of Revenue. Attach your IRS Determination Letter and Letter of Incorporation.

Step-13: Charitable Solicitation Registration

This is yet another area where it varies between states, but most require it on an annual basis. This means you need to register with the state before fundraising from any resident of the state. Depending on the scope of your organization you may need to register in other states as well.

Overseen By: Georgia Professional Licensing Boards and Securities Division.

Exemptions:
1. Less than $25,000 nationwide contributions for preceding and current calendar years
2. Religious organizations
3. Educational institutions
4. Professional associations
5. Fraternal and social organizations
6. Political groups
7. Appeals for individuals
8. Local affiliates

To file in Georgia, you need to do the following:

Form: Charitable Organization Registration Form (URS) with Control Persons Form or Form C-100: Charitable Organization Registration
Submit To: Georgia Professional Licensing Boards and Securities Division
How to File: Mail
Cost: $35

Additional Notes:
- Attach all necessary documents
- Requires the notarized signature of an authorized executive officer

Step-14: Business Licenses and Permits

From here you will be all set to start your nonprofit. However, the work isn't over yet. You'll also need to stay in compliance with your nonprofit. Next, consider your required annual filings to remain legal.

Annual Renewal

1. IRS Renewals
   a. IRS Form 990
   b. Due the 15th day of the 5th month following the end of the taxable year.
2. Georgia corporate income tax exemption renewal
   a. Filed with Georgia Department of Revenue
   b. File a copy for federal form 990 to Form 660-T
   c. Due four and a half months after the end of the fiscal year
3. Georgia has no requirement for sale tax exemption renewal. However you'll need to present your IRS Determination Letter on request.
4. Georgia requires an annual registration
   a. Filed with the Georgia Secretary of State
   b. File a copy of the Annual Registration
   c. Filed by mail or online
   d. Costs $30
   e. Due annually by April 1st
   f. $25 late filing fee
5. Charitable Solicitation Renewal
   a. Filed with the Georgia Professional Licensing Boards and Securities Division
   b. Form Charitable Organization Renewal
   c. Filed by mail
   d. Costs $20
   e. The license must be renewed biennially by the registration date
   f. Include all necessary forms including financial statements

HAWAII

Step-1: Name Your Nonprofit

The name of your nonprofit will establish its brand and will allow you to incorporate with the state. The name you choose cannot conflict with any other organization registered within the state of Hawaii. Make sure the name you choose is available and meets all state requirement. Search through the Hawaii Business Registration Division.

Step-2: Get Initial Directors and Incorporators

The incorporate is the individual who signs the Articles of Incorporation for your business. You will need at least one incorporator, but you can have additional. The directors are the governing body of your nonprofit and are stakeholders in the purpose and success of your nonprofit. You should have at least three directors who are unrelated individuals in order to meet IRS requirements. You'll also want to meet age and residency requirements.

Step-3: Selected a Registered Agent

The registered agent is responsible for receiving legal notices for your nonprofit. A registered agent needs to be physically living in the state and maintain an office open during regular business hours.

Step-4: Articles of Incorporation

The articles of incorporation are the official creation of your nonprofit. They show where and when the nonprofit was formed and provide the necessary information to verify the nonprofits existence. Make sure your articles of incorporation meet state and IRS requirement.

Form: Articles of Incorporation
Submit To: Hawaii Business Registration Division
How to File: Mail, fax, in person or online
Cost: $26. Optional $25 expedite.
Time Frame: About 7-14 days by mail. About 3-5 days by fax, in person or online. About 1-3 days online with an expedite fee.

Step-5: Get an Employer Identification Number (EIN)

This is a unique nine-digit number that the IRS assigned to identify your nonprofit. Your EIN is then used to open a bank account, apply for 501(c)(3) status and submit 990 IRS returns.

Form: IRS Form SS-4
Submit To: Internal Revenue Service (IRS)
How to File: Mail, phone, fax or online
Cost: $0
Time Frame: By phone or online is immediate, by fax is 4 days and by mail is 4-5 weeks.

Additional Notes:
- Print EIN before the closing session

Step-6: Storing Records

As you start a nonprofit, you will be faced with a number of official documents. Be sure you organize and store all of these records together for easy access later.

Step-7: Initial Governing Policies and Documents

The governing document for your nonprofit is your bylaws since they serve as the operating manual for your organization and need to be consistent with both the law and

your articles of incorporation. The first meeting of your Board of Directors should be to review and ratify the bylaws.

You should also create and adopt a conflict of interest policy. This will guide you in what to do if someone in a key position within your nonprofit has competing interests and makes a decision that benefits themselves while harming your nonprofit. Organizational interests should be prioritized ahead of personal interests. All conflicts should be disclosed immediately.

Both the bylaws and the conflict of interest policy will need to be approved and adopted before applying to the IRS for 501(c)(3) status.

Step-8: Board of Directors Organizational Meeting

This initial meeting is the most productive and important one. You will approve bylaws, adopt the conflict of interest policy, elect directors, appoint officers and approve any resolutions like opening a bank account. Be sure to record the decisions made in meeting minutes.

Step-9: State Tax Identification Numbers and Accounts

Incorporating a nonprofit means, you will follow all state laws. Requirements vary by state so check with your individual state first.

Alabama has a consolidated state tax registration application:

Form: BB-1: State of Hawaii Basic Business Application
Submit To: State of Hawaii - Department of Taxation
How to File: Mail or online
Cost: $20

Step-10: File for 501(c) Status

This can seem like one of the most difficult steps in starting your nonprofit, but it also offers many benefits. After applying and submitting your documents, the IRS will give you a Determination Letter that officially recognizes your tax-exempt status.

Form: IRS Form 1023, Form 1023-EZ or Form 1024
Submit To: Internal Revenue Service (IRS)
How to File: Mail
Cost: $275 for Form 1023-EZ and $600 for Form 1023
Time Frame: Less than a month for Form 1023-EZ and 3-6 months for Form 1023

Step-11: State Tax Exemption

Once you have your IRS Determination Letter, you next need to figure out your state's requirements for tax-exempt status. This is another area that varies by state. You may also need to do periodic renewals for tax-exempt status.

In Hawaii, you obtain your state income tax exemption when you get your IRS Determination Letter.

For general excise tax exemption in Hawaii you need to do the following:

Form: G-6: Application for Exemption from General Excise Taxes
Submit To: Hawaii Department of Taxation
Cost: $20

Step-12: Charitable Solicitation Registration
This is yet another area where it varies between states, but most require it on an annual basis. This means you need to register with the state before fundraising from any

resident of the state. Depending on the scope of your organization you may need to register in other states as well.

Overseen By: Hawaii Tax and Charities Division

Exemptions:
1. Less than $25,000 contributions annually
2. Religious organizations
3. Educational institutions
4. Membership organizations
5. Nonprofit hospitals
6. Government agencies
7. Fundraisers not involving paid solicitors

To file in Hawaii, you need to do the following:

Submit To: Hawaii Tax and Charities Division
How to File: Online
Cost: $0

Additional Notes:
- The signatures of two officers or directors are required, and they must have their own login IDs.

Step-13: Business Licenses and Permits
From here you will be all set to start your nonprofit. However, the work isn't over yet. You'll also need to stay in compliance with your nonprofit. Next, consider your required annual filings to remain legal.

Annual Renewal

1. IRS Renewals
    a. IRS Form 990
    b. Due the 15th day of the 5th month following the end of the taxable year.
2. Hawaii Corporate Tax Returns
    a. Filed with the Hawaii Department of Taxation
    b. File Form G-45: General Excise / Use Tax Return and G-49: General Excise / Use Annual Return and Reconciliation
    c. Due monthly, quarterly or semi-annually based on instructions and the 20th day of the 4th month following the close of the taxable year
3. Hawaii has no corporate tax exemption renewal.
4. Hawaii has no sales tax exemption renewal.
5. Hawaii requires the filing of an annual report
    a. Filed with Hawaii Business Registration Division
    b. File Form D2
    c. File by mail, in person or online
    d. Costs $5
    e. Annual reports are due during the quarter that contains the registration anniversary date
    f. Expedited processing is available for an additional $25 fee
6. Charitable Solicitation Renewal
    a. Filed with the Hawaii Tax and Charities Division
    b. IRS Form 990
    c. Filed by online
    d. Costs $10-750 depending on annual gross revenue
    e. Due annually on the same day as IRS Form 990 or four and a half months after the close of the fiscal year

IDAHO

Step-1: Name Your Nonprofit

The name of your nonprofit will establish its brand and will allow you to incorporate with the state. The name you choose cannot conflict with any other organization registered within the state of Idaho. Make sure the name you choose is available and meets all state requirement. Search through the Idaho Secretary of State.

Step-2: Get Initial Directors and Incorporators

The incorporate is the individual who signs the Articles of Incorporation for your business. You will need at least one incorporator, but you can have additional. The directors are the governing body of your nonprofit and are stakeholders in the purpose and success of your nonprofit. You should have at least three directors who are unrelated individuals in order to meet IRS requirements. You'll also want to meet age and residency requirements.

Step-3: Selected a Registered Agent

The registered agent is responsible for receiving legal notices for your nonprofit. A registered agent needs to be physically living in the state and maintain an office open during regular business hours.

Step-4: Articles of Incorporation

The articles of incorporation are the official creation of your nonprofit. They show where and when the nonprofit was formed and provide the necessary information to verify the nonprofits existence. Make sure your articles of incorporation meet state and IRS requirement.

Form: Nonprofit - Articles of Incorporation
Submit To: Idaho Secretary of State
How to File: Mail or in person
Cost: $30. Optional $20 expedite.
Time Frame: About 1 week. About 1 day expedite.

Additional Notes:
- Submit two copies

Step-5: Get an Employer Identification Number (EIN)

This is a unique nine-digit number that the IRS assigned to identify your nonprofit. Your EIN is then used to open a bank account, apply for 501(c)(3) status and submit 990 IRS returns.

Form: IRS Form SS-4
Submit To: Internal Revenue Service (IRS)
How to File: Mail, phone, fax or online
Cost: $0
Time Frame: By phone or online is immediate, by fax is 4 days and by mail is 4-5 weeks.

Additional Notes:
- Print EIN before the closing session

Step-6: Storing Records

As you start a nonprofit, you will be faced with a number of official documents. Be sure you organize and store all of these records together for easy access later.

Step-7: Initial Governing Policies and Documents

The governing document for your nonprofit is your bylaws since they serve as the operating manual for your organization and need to be consistent with both the law and your articles of incorporation. The first meeting of your Board of Directors should be to review and ratify the bylaws.

You should also create and adopt a conflict of interest policy. This will guide you in what to do if someone in a key position within your nonprofit has competing interests and makes a decision that benefits themselves while harming your nonprofit. Organizational interests should be prioritized ahead of personal interests. All conflicts should be disclosed immediately.

Both the bylaws and the conflict of interest policy will need to be approved and adopted before applying to the IRS for 501(c)(3) status.

Step-8: Board of Directors Organizational Meeting

This initial meeting is the most productive and important one. You will approve bylaws, adopt the conflict of interest policy, elect directors, appoint officers and approve any resolutions like opening a bank account. Be sure to record the decisions made in meeting minutes.

Step-9: State Tax Identification Numbers and Accounts

Incorporating a nonprofit means, you will follow all state laws. Requirements vary by state so check with your individual state first.

For an Idaho nonprofit making retail sales, you'll need a seller's permit. If you plan to have employees, you'll need a withholding account. File online for free through the Idaho State Tax Commission.

Step-10: File for 501(c) Status

This can seem like one of the most difficult steps in starting your nonprofit, but it also offers many benefits. After applying and submitting your documents, the IRS will give you a Determination Letter that officially recognizes your tax-exempt status.

Form: IRS Form 1023, Form 1023-EZ or Form 1024
Submit To: Internal Revenue Service (IRS)
How to File: Mail
Cost: $275 for Form 1023-EZ and $600 for Form 1023
Time Frame: Less than a month for Form 1023-EZ and 3-6 months for Form 1023

Step-11: State Tax Exemption

Once you have your IRS Determination Letter, you next need to figure out your state's requirements for tax-exempt status. This is another area that varies by state. You may also need to do periodic renewals for tax-exempt status.

In Idaho, you obtain your state income tax exemption when you get your IRS Determination Letter.

For state sales tax exemption in Idaho, you need to apply through the Idaho State Tax Commission.

Step-12: Charitable Solicitation Registration
This is yet another area where it varies between states, but most require it on an annual basis. This means you need to register with the state before fundraising from any resident of the state. Depending on the scope of your organization you may need to register in other states as well.

This registration isn't required in Idaho. The Idaho Charitable Solicitation Act prohibits any false, deceptive, misleading, unfair or unconscionable acts or practices when soliciting in Idaho. For telephone soliciting, you need to register with the attorney general 10 days prior.

Step-13: Business Licenses and Permits

From here you will be all set to start your nonprofit. However, the work isn't over yet. You'll also need to stay in compliance with your nonprofit. Next, consider your required annual filings to remain legal.

Annual Renewal

1. IRS Renewals
    a. IRS Form 990
    b. Due the 15th day of the 5th month following the end of the taxable year.
2. Idaho has no renewal requirements for corporate income tax exemption.
3. Idaho doesn't offer sales tax exemptions to nonprofits.
4. Idaho requires an annual report
    a. Filed with Idaho Secretary of State
    b. Filed online
    c. Costs $0
    d. Due the last day of registration anniversary month.

ILLINOIS

Step-1: Name Your Nonprofit

The name of your nonprofit will establish its brand and will allow you to incorporate with the state. The name you choose cannot conflict with any other organization registered within the state of Illinois. Make sure the name you choose is available and meets all state requirement. Search through the Illinois Secretary of State - Business Services Department.

Step-2: Get Initial Directors and Incorporators

The incorporate is the individual who signs the Articles of Incorporation for your business. You will need at least one incorporator, but you can have additional. The directors are the governing body of your nonprofit and are stakeholders in the purpose and success of your nonprofit. You should have at least three directors who are unrelated individuals in order to meet IRS requirements. You'll also want to meet age and residency requirements.

Step-3: Selected a Registered Agent

The registered agent is responsible for receiving legal notices for your nonprofit. A registered agent needs to be physically living in the state and maintain an office open during regular business hours.

Step-4: Articles of Incorporation

The articles of incorporation are the official creation of your nonprofit. They show where and when the nonprofit was formed and provide the necessary information to verify the

nonprofits existence. Make sure your articles of incorporation meet state and IRS requirement.

Form: NFP 102.10: Articles of Incorporation
Submit To: Illinois Secretary of State - Business Services Department
How to File: Mail, fax with a prepaid account or online
Cost: $50 by mail. $77.75 online. Optional $100 expedite.
Time Frame: About 2 weeks by mail or fax. About 1-5 days online with expedite.

Additional Notes:
- When filing by mail, you need to submit two articles of incorporation, an original in black ink and a copy.

Step-5: Get an Employer Identification Number (EIN)

This is a unique nine-digit number that the IRS assigned to identify your nonprofit. Your EIN is then used to open a bank account, apply for 501(c)(3) status and submit 990 IRS returns.

Form: IRS Form SS-4
Submit To: Internal Revenue Service (IRS)
How to File: Mail, phone, fax or online
Cost: $0
Time Frame: By phone or online is immediate, by fax is 4 days and by mail is 4-5 weeks.

Additional Notes:
- Print EIN before the closing session

Step-6: Storing Records

As you start a nonprofit, you will be faced with a number of official documents. Be sure you organize and store all of these records together for easy access later.

Step-7: Initial Governing Policies and Documents

The governing document for your nonprofit is your bylaws since they serve as the operating manual for your organization and need to be consistent with both the law and your articles of incorporation. The first meeting of your Board of Directors should be to review and ratify the bylaws.

You should also create and adopt a conflict of interest policy. This will guide you in what to do if someone in a key position within your nonprofit has competing interests and makes a decision that benefits themselves while harming your nonprofit. Organizational interests should be prioritized ahead of personal interests. All conflicts should be disclosed immediately.

Both the bylaws and the conflict of interest policy will need to be approved and adopted before applying to the IRS for 501(c)(3) status.

Step-8: Board of Directors Organizational Meeting

This initial meeting is the most productive and important one. You will approve bylaws, adopt the conflict of interest policy, elect directors, appoint officers and approve any resolutions like opening a bank account. Be sure to record the decisions made in meeting minutes.

Step-9: State Tax Identification Numbers and Accounts

Incorporating a nonprofit means, you will follow all state laws. Requirements vary by state so check with your individual state first.

Illinois has a consolidated state tax registration application:

Form: REG-1: Illinois Business Registration Application
Submit To: Illinois Department of Revenue
How to File: Mail or online
Cost: Varies depending on tax accounts needed

Step-10: File for 501(c) Status

This can seem like one of the most difficult steps in starting your nonprofit, but it also offers many benefits. After applying and submitting your documents, the IRS will give you a Determination Letter that officially recognizes your tax-exempt status.

Form: IRS Form 1023, Form 1023-EZ or Form 1024
Submit To: Internal Revenue Service (IRS)
How to File: Mail
Cost: $275 for Form 1023-EZ and $600 for Form 1023
Time Frame: Less than a month for Form 1023-EZ and 3-6 months for Form 1023

Step-11: State Tax Exemption

Once you have your IRS Determination Letter, you next need to figure out your state's requirements for tax-exempt status. This is another area that varies by state. You may also need to do periodic renewals for tax-exempt status.

In Illinois, you obtain your state income tax exemption when you get your IRS Determination Letter.

For state sales tax exemption in Illinois you need to do the following:
Form: STAX-1: Application for Sales Tax Exemption

Submit To: Illinois Department of Revenue

Cost: $0

Step-12: Charitable Solicitation Registration

This is yet another area where it varies between states, but most require it on an annual basis. This means you need to register with the state before fundraising from any resident of the state. Depending on the scope of your organization you may need to register in other states as well.

Overseen By: Illinois Attorney General - Charitable Trust Bureau

To file in Illinois, you need to do the following:

Form: A submission package including:
1. Form CO-1: Registration Statement
2. List of all directors, officers and/or trustees with names, mailing addresses and daytime phone numbers
3. IRS Determination Letter or IRS 1023 or explanation letter
4. Copies of contracts with Professional Fund Raisers
5. Form CO-3: Religious Organization Exemption Form
6. Articles of Incorporation and all amendments
7. Bylaws
8. Form CO-2 or AG990-IL depending on how long your nonprofit has been in business

Submit To: Illinois Attorney General - Charitable Trust Bureau

How to File: Mail

Cost: $15

Additional Notes:

- Attach all necessary documents
- Must be signed by the CFO and President or other authorized officer. Must be two individuals.
- Signatures don't have to be notarized

Step-13: Business Licenses and Permits

From here you will be all set to start your nonprofit. However, the work isn't over yet. You'll also need to stay in compliance with your nonprofit. Next, consider your required annual filings to remain legal.

Annual Renewal

1. IRS Renewals
    a. IRS Form 990
    b. Due the 15th day of the 5th month following the end of the taxable year.
2. Illinois has no renewal requirements for corporate income tax exemption.
3. Illinois Sales Tax Exemption Renewal
    a. Filed with the Illinois Department of Revenue
    b. File online for free
    c. Due every 5 years from date of issue
4. Illinois requires an annual report
    a. Filed with the Illinois Secretary of State - Business Services Department
    b. File Domestic/Foreign Corporation Annual Report
    c. Filed by mail or online
    d. Costs $10 with $50 expedite fee when filing online
    e. Due annually at the end of the anniversary month
    f. $3 late fee
5. Charitable Solicitation Renewal
    a. Filed with the Illinois Attorney General - Charitable Trust Bureau

b. Form AG990-IL: Illinois Charitable Organization Supplement
c. Filed by mail
d. Costs $15
e. $100 late fee
f. Due 6 months after close of the fiscal year
g. Include all attachments including financial audit if requested

INDIANA

Step-1: Name Your Nonprofit

The name of your nonprofit will establish its brand and will allow you to incorporate with the state. The name you choose cannot conflict with any other organization registered within the state of Indiana. Make sure the name you choose is available and meets all state requirement. Search through the Indiana Secretary of State - Business Services Division.

Step-2: Get Initial Directors and Incorporators

The incorporate is the individual who signs the Articles of Incorporation for your business. You will need at least one incorporator, but you can have additional. The directors are the governing body of your nonprofit and are stakeholders in the purpose and success of your nonprofit. You should have at least three directors who are unrelated individuals in order to meet IRS requirements. You'll also want to meet age and residency requirements.

Step-3: Selected a Registered Agent

The registered agent is responsible for receiving legal notices for your nonprofit. A registered agent needs to be physically living in the state and maintain an office open during regular business hours.

Step-4: Articles of Incorporation

The articles of incorporation are the official creation of your nonprofit. They show where and when the nonprofit was formed and provide the necessary information to verify the

nonprofits existence. Make sure your articles of incorporation meet state and IRS requirement.

Form: Articles of Incorporation 4162
Submit To: Indiana Secretary of State - Business Services Division
How to File: Mail, in person or online
Cost: $50
Time Frame: About 15 minutes online. About 24 hours in person. About 5-7 days by mail.

Additional Notes:
- Send one original and one copy.

Step-5: Get an Employer Identification Number (EIN)

This is a unique nine-digit number that the IRS assigned to identify your nonprofit. Your EIN is then used to open a bank account, apply for 501(c)(3) status and submit 990 IRS returns.

Form: IRS Form SS-4
Submit To: Internal Revenue Service (IRS)
How to File: Mail, phone, fax or online
Cost: $0
Time Frame: By phone or online is immediate, by fax is 4 days and by mail is 4-5 weeks.

Additional Notes:
- Print EIN before the closing session

Step-6: Storing Records

As you start a nonprofit, you will be faced with a number of official documents. Be sure you organize and store all of these records together for easy access later.

Step-7: Initial Governing Policies and Documents

The governing document for your nonprofit is your bylaws since they serve as the operating manual for your organization and need to be consistent with both the law and your articles of incorporation. The first meeting of your Board of Directors should be to review and ratify the bylaws.

You should also create and adopt a conflict of interest policy. This will guide you in what to do if someone in a key position within your nonprofit has competing interests and makes a decision that benefits themselves while harming your nonprofit. Organizational interests should be prioritized ahead of personal interests. All conflicts should be disclosed immediately.

Both the bylaws and the conflict of interest policy will need to be approved and adopted before applying to the IRS for 501(c)(3) status.

Step-8: Board of Directors Organizational Meeting
This initial meeting is the most productive and important one. You will approve bylaws, adopt the conflict of interest policy, elect directors, appoint officers and approve any resolutions like opening a bank account. Be sure to record the decisions made in meeting minutes.

Step-9: State Tax Identification Numbers and Accounts

Incorporating a nonprofit means, you will follow all state laws. Requirements vary by state so check with your individual state first.

Indiana has a consolidated state tax registration application:

Form: BT-1: Indiana Business Tax Application
Submit To: Indiana Department of Revenue
How to File: Online
Cost: $0. A sales tax license if $25.
Time Frame: Varies

Step-10: File for 501(c) Status

This can seem like one of the most difficult steps in starting your nonprofit, but it also offers many benefits. After applying and submitting your documents, the IRS will give you a Determination Letter that officially recognizes your tax-exempt status.

Form: IRS Form 1023, Form 1023-EZ or Form 1024
Submit To: Internal Revenue Service (IRS)
How to File: Mail
Cost: $275 for Form 1023-EZ and $600 for Form 1023
Time Frame: Less than a month for Form 1023-EZ and 3-6 months for Form 1023

Step-11: State Tax Exemption

Once you have your IRS Determination Letter, you next need to figure out your state's requirements for tax-exempt status. This is another area that varies by state. You may also need to do periodic renewals for tax-exempt status.

For income tax exemption in Indiana:

Form: NP-20A: Nonprofit Application for Sales Tax Exemption
Submit To: Indiana Department of Revenue

Cost: $0

Additional Notes:
- Attach an IRS Determination Letter
- The application must be within 120 days of incorporation

For state sales tax exemption in Indiana you need to do the following:

Form: NP-20: Nonprofit Application for Sales Tax Exemption
Submit To: Indiana Department of Revenue
Cost: $0

Additional Notes:
- Attach an IRS Determination Letter
- The application must be within 120 days of incorporation

Step-12: Charitable Solicitation Registration

This license is not required in Indiana. Some counties and municipalities may require registration.

Step-13: Business Licenses and Permits

From here you will be all set to start your nonprofit. However, the work isn't over yet. You'll also need to stay in compliance with your nonprofit. Next, consider your required annual filings to remain legal.

Annual Renewal

1. IRS Renewals
    a. IRS Form 990

    b. Due the 15th day of the 5th month following the end of the taxable year.
2. Indiana Corporate Tax Exemption Renewal
    a. Filed with the Indiana Department of Revenue
    b. Form NP-20: Indiana Nonprofit Organization Annual Report
    c. Cost $0
    d. Due annually on the 15th day of the 5th month at fiscal year-end
3. Indiana Sales Tax Exemption Renewal
    a. Filed with the Indiana Department of Revenue
    b. Form NP-20: Indiana Nonprofit Organization Annual Report
    c. Cost $0
    d. Due annually within four and a half months of fiscal year end
4. Indiana requires an annual report
    a. Filed with Indiana Secretary of State - Business Services Division
    b. Filed the Indiana Business Entity Report
    c. Filed by mail or online
    d. Costs $20 by mail or $22 online
    e. Due biennially by the end of the anniversary month

IOWA

Step-1: Name Your Nonprofit

The name of your nonprofit will establish its brand and will allow you to incorporate with the state. The name you choose cannot conflict with any other organization registered within the state of Iowa. Make sure the name you choose is available and meets all state requirement. Search through the Iowa Secretary of State.

Step-2: Get Initial Directors and Incorporators

The incorporate is the individual who signs the Articles of Incorporation for your business. You will need at least one incorporator, but you can have additional. The directors are the governing body of your nonprofit and are stakeholders in the purpose and success of your nonprofit. You should have at least three directors who are unrelated individuals in order to meet IRS requirements. You'll also want to meet age and residency requirements.

Step-3: Selected a Registered Agent

The registered agent is responsible for receiving legal notices for your nonprofit. A registered agent needs to be physically living in the state and maintain an office open during regular business hours.

Step-4: Articles of Incorporation

The articles of incorporation are the official creation of your nonprofit. They show where and when the nonprofit was formed and provide the necessary information to verify the nonprofits existence. Make sure your articles of incorporation meet state and IRS requirement.

Form: Articles of Incorporation
Submit To: Iowa Secretary of State
How to File: Mail, fax or online
Cost: $20
Time Frame: About 1-2 days

Step-5: Get an Employer Identification Number (EIN)

This is a unique nine-digit number that the IRS assigned to identify your nonprofit. Your EIN is then used to open a bank account, apply for 501(c)(3) status and submit 990 IRS returns.

Form: IRS Form SS-4
Submit To: Internal Revenue Service (IRS)
How to File: Mail, phone, fax or online
Cost: $0
Time Frame: By phone or online is immediate, by fax is 4 days and by mail is 4-5 weeks.

Additional Notes:
- Print EIN before the closing session

Step-6: Storing Records

As you start a nonprofit, you will be faced with a number of official documents. Be sure you organize and store all of these records together for easy access later.

Step-7: Initial Governing Policies and Documents

The governing document for your nonprofit is your bylaws since they serve as the operating manual for your organization and need to be consistent with both the law and

your articles of incorporation. The first meeting of your Board of Directors should be to review and ratify the bylaws.

You should also create and adopt a conflict of interest policy. This will guide you in what to do if someone in a key position within your nonprofit has competing interests and makes a decision that benefits themselves while harming your nonprofit. Organizational interests should be prioritized ahead of personal interests. All conflicts should be disclosed immediately.

Both the bylaws and the conflict of interest policy will need to be approved and adopted before applying to the IRS for 501(c)(3) status.

Step-8: Board of Directors Organizational Meeting

This initial meeting is the most productive and important one. You will approve bylaws, adopt the conflict of interest policy, elect directors, appoint officers and approve any resolutions like opening a bank account. Be sure to record the decisions made in meeting minutes.

Step-9: State Tax Identification Numbers and Accounts

Incorporating a nonprofit means, you will follow all state laws. Requirements vary by state so check with your individual state first.

To file in Iowa:

Form: 78-005a: Iowa Business Tax Registration
Submit To: Iowa Department of Revenue
How to File: Mail or online
Cost: Varies based on accounts/licenses

Time Frame: About 4-5 weeks

Step-10: File for 501(c) Status

This can seem like one of the most difficult steps in starting your nonprofit, but it also offers many benefits. After applying and submitting your documents, the IRS will give you a Determination Letter that officially recognizes your tax-exempt status.

Form: IRS Form 1023, Form 1023-EZ or Form 1024
Submit To: Internal Revenue Service (IRS)
How to File: Mail
Cost: $275 for Form 1023-EZ and $600 for Form 1023
Time Frame: Less than a month for Form 1023-EZ and 3-6 months for Form 1023

Step-11: State Tax Exemption

Once you have your IRS Determination Letter, you next need to figure out your state's requirements for tax-exempt status. This is another area that varies by state. You may also need to do periodic renewals for tax-exempt status.

In Iowa, you obtain your state income tax exemption when you get your IRS Determination Letter.

Iowa doesn't offer sales tax exemption to nonprofits.

Step-12: Charitable Solicitation Registration
This is yet another area where it varies between states, but most require it on an annual basis. This means you need to register with the state before fundraising from any resident of the state. Depending on the scope of your organization you may need to register in other states as well.

This license is not required in the state of Iowa.

Step-13: Business Licenses and Permits

From here you will be all set to start your nonprofit. However, the work isn't over yet. You'll also need to stay in compliance with your nonprofit. Next, consider your required annual filings to remain legal.

Annual Renewal

1. IRS Renewals
    a. IRS Form 990
    b. Due the 15th day of the 5th month following the end of the taxable year.
2. Iowa has no renewal requirements for corporate income tax exemption.
3. Iowa doesn't offer sales tax exemption.
4. Iowa requires a biennial report
    a. Filed by mail or online
    b. Filed with the Iowa Secretary of State
    c. Costs $0
    d. Due by April 1st in odd years
    e. No late fee. Your business is dissolved or revoked in a few months if late.
    f. May be filed by anyone with authority
    g. Does not require original signatures

KANSAS

Step-1: Name Your Nonprofit

The name of your nonprofit will establish its brand and will allow you to incorporate with the state. The name you choose cannot conflict with any other organization registered within the state of Kansas. Make sure the name you choose is available and meets all state requirement. Search through the Kansas Secretary of State.

Step-2: Get Initial Directors and Incorporators

The incorporate is the individual who signs the Articles of Incorporation for your business. You will need at least one incorporator, but you can have additional. The directors are the governing body of your nonprofit and are stakeholders in the purpose and success of your nonprofit. You should have at least three directors who are unrelated individuals in order to meet IRS requirements. You'll also want to meet age and residency requirements.

Step-3: Selected a Registered Agent

The registered agent is responsible for receiving legal notices for your nonprofit. A registered agent needs to be physically living in the state and maintain an office open during regular business hours.

Step-4: Articles of Incorporation

The articles of incorporation are the official creation of your nonprofit. They show where and when the nonprofit was formed and provide the necessary information to verify the nonprofits existence. Make sure your articles of incorporation meet state and IRS requirement.

Form: CN: Not-for-Profit Corporation Articles of Incorporation
Submit To: Kansas Secretary of State
How to File: Mail, fax, in person or online
Cost: $20. Optional $20 expedite.
Time Frame: Immediate online. About 4 days by paper. About one day by paper with expediting fees.

Step-5: Get an Employer Identification Number (EIN)

This is a unique nine-digit number that the IRS assigned to identify your nonprofit. Your EIN is then used to open a bank account, apply for 501(c)(3) status and submit 990 IRS returns.

Form: IRS Form SS-4
Submit To: Internal Revenue Service (IRS)
How to File: Mail, phone, fax or online
Cost: $0
Time Frame: By phone or online is immediate, by fax is 4 days and by mail is 4-5 weeks.

Additional Notes:
- Print EIN before the closing session

Step-6: Storing Records

As you start a nonprofit, you will be faced with a number of official documents. Be sure you organize and store all of these records together for easy access later.

Step-7: Initial Governing Policies and Documents

The governing document for your nonprofit is your bylaws since they serve as the operating manual for your organization and need to be consistent with both the law and your articles of incorporation. The first meeting of your Board of Directors should be to review and ratify the bylaws.

You should also create and adopt a conflict of interest policy. This will guide you in what to do if someone in a key position within your nonprofit has competing interests and makes a decision that benefits themselves while harming your nonprofit. Organizational interests should be prioritized ahead of personal interests. All conflicts should be disclosed immediately.

Both the bylaws and the conflict of interest policy will need to be approved and adopted before applying to the IRS for 501(c)(3) status.

Step-8: Board of Directors Organizational Meeting

This initial meeting is the most productive and important one. You will approve bylaws, adopt the conflict of interest policy, elect directors, appoint officers and approve any resolutions like opening a bank account. Be sure to record the decisions made in meeting minutes.

Step-9: State Tax Identification Numbers and Accounts

Incorporating a nonprofit means, you will follow all state laws. Requirements vary by state so check with your individual state first.

In Kansas you must register since you are required to pay tax:

Form: CR-16: Kansas Business Tax Application
Submit To: Kansas Department of Revenue

How to File: Mail or online

Cost: Varies based on accounts and licenses

Step-10: File for 501(c) Status

This can seem like one of the most difficult steps in starting your nonprofit, but it also offers many benefits. After applying and submitting your documents, the IRS will give you a Determination Letter that officially recognizes your tax-exempt status.

Form: IRS Form 1023, Form 1023-EZ or Form 1024
Submit To: Internal Revenue Service (IRS)
How to File: Mail
Cost: $275 for Form 1023-EZ and $600 for Form 1023
Time Frame: Less than a month for Form 1023-EZ and 3-6 months for Form 1023

Step-11: State Tax Exemption

Once you have your IRS Determination Letter, you next need to figure out your state's requirements for tax-exempt status. This is another area that varies by state. You may also need to do periodic renewals for tax-exempt status.

In Kansas, you obtain your state income tax exemption when you get your IRS Determination Letter.

For state sales tax exemption in Kansas:

Submit To: Kansas Department of Revenue
Cost: $0

Step-12: Charitable Solicitation Registration

This is yet another area where it varies between states, but most require it on an annual basis. This means you need to register with the state before fundraising from any resident of the state. Depending on the scope of your organization you may need to register in other states as well.

Overseen By: Kansas Secretary of State – Charities

Exemptions:
1. Less than $10,000 nationwide contributions a year with all fundraising done by volunteers
2. Less than 100 people are solicited a year
3. Religious organizations
4. Educational institutions
5. Health organizations
6. Membership organizations
7. Appeals for individuals
8. Public foundations

To file in Kansas, you need to do the following:

Form: SC: Registration Statement for Solicitations
Submit To: Kansas Secretary of State - Charities
How to File: Mail
Cost: $35

Additional Notes:
- Attach all necessary documents
- Must be signed by the CFO and another authorized officer. Must be two individuals.
- Notarization is not needed.

Step-13: Business Licenses and Permits

From here you will be all set to start your nonprofit. However, the work isn't over yet. You'll also need to stay in compliance with your nonprofit. Next, consider your required annual filings to remain legal.

Annual Renewal

1. IRS Renewals
    a. IRS Form 990
    b. Due the 15th day of the 5th month following the end of the taxable year.
2. Kansas has no renewal requirements for corporate income tax exemption.
3. Kansas Sales Tax Exemption Renewal
    a. Filed with the Kansas Department of Revenue
    b. Due by the date on the exemption certificate
    c. Filed online
4. Kansas requires an annual report
    a. Filed with the Kansas Secretary of State
    b. Form Non-for-Profit Corporation Annual Report
    c. Filed by mail or online
    d. Costs $40
    e. Due annually on the 15th day of the 6th month after the close of the fiscal year
    f. Your business will be forfeited if you are 90 days late
    g. The paper form must be signed by a member, partner or officer
    h. The form must have original signatures
5. Charitable Solicitation Renewal
    a. Filed with the Kansas Secretary of State - Charities
    b. Form SC: Registration Statement for Solicitations
    c. Filed by mail

d. Costs $35
e. Due annually six months after the close of the fiscal year
f. Include all required documents
g. Must be signed by the CFO and another authorized officer. Must be two individuals.
h. Notarization is not needed

KENTUCKY

Step-1: Name Your Nonprofit

The name of your nonprofit will establish its brand and will allow you to incorporate with the state. The name you choose cannot conflict with any other organization registered within the state of Kentucky. Make sure the name you choose is available and meets all state requirement. Search through the Kentucky Secretary of State.

Step-2: Get Initial Directors and Incorporators

The incorporate is the individual who signs the Articles of Incorporation for your business. You will need at least one incorporator, but you can have additional. The directors are the governing body of your nonprofit and are stakeholders in the purpose and success of your nonprofit. You should have at least three directors who are unrelated individuals in order to meet IRS requirements. You'll also want to meet age and residency requirements.

Step-3: Selected a Registered Agent

The registered agent is responsible for receiving legal notices for your nonprofit. A registered agent needs to be physically living in the state and maintain an office open during regular business hours.

Step-4: Articles of Incorporation

The articles of incorporation are the official creation of your nonprofit. They show where and when the nonprofit was formed and provide the necessary information to verify the nonprofits existence. Make sure your articles of incorporation meet state and IRS requirement.

Form: Articles of Incorporation
Submit To: Kentucky Secretary of State
How to File: Mail, in person or online
Cost: $8
Time Frame: About 3-5 days by mail or online. While you wait if filed in person

Step-5: Get an Employer Identification Number (EIN)

This is a unique nine-digit number that the IRS assigned to identify your nonprofit. Your EIN is then used to open a bank account, apply for 501(c)(3) status and submit 990 IRS returns.

Form: IRS Form SS-4
Submit To: Internal Revenue Service (IRS)
How to File: Mail, phone, fax or online
Cost: $0
Time Frame: By phone or online is immediate, by fax is 4 days and by mail is 4-5 weeks.

Additional Notes:
- Print EIN before the closing session

Step-6: Storing Records

As you start a nonprofit, you will be faced with a number of official documents. Be sure you organize and store all of these records together for easy access later.

Step-7: Initial Governing Policies and Documents

The governing document for your nonprofit is your bylaws since they serve as the operating manual for your organization and need to be consistent with both the law and

your articles of incorporation. The first meeting of your Board of Directors should be to review and ratify the bylaws.

You should also create and adopt a conflict of interest policy. This will guide you in what to do if someone in a key position within your nonprofit has competing interests and makes a decision that benefits themselves while harming your nonprofit. Organizational interests should be prioritized ahead of personal interests. All conflicts should be disclosed immediately.

Both the bylaws and the conflict of interest policy will need to be approved and adopted before applying to the IRS for 501(c)(3) status.

Step-8: Board of Directors Organizational Meeting

This initial meeting is the most productive and important one. You will approve bylaws, adopt the conflict of interest policy, elect directors, appoint officers and approve any resolutions like opening a bank account. Be sure to record the decisions made in meeting minutes.

Step-9: State Tax Identification Numbers and Accounts

Incorporating a nonprofit means, you will follow all state laws. Requirements vary by state so check with your individual state first.

In Kentucky registration is required within 30 days of incorporation:

Form: 10A100: Kentucky Tax Registration Application
Submit To: Kentucky Department of Revenue
How to File: Mail or online
Cost: $0

Time Frame: About 5-10 days

Step-10: File for 501(c) Status

This can seem like one of the most difficult steps in starting your nonprofit, but it also offers many benefits. After applying and submitting your documents, the IRS will give you a Determination Letter that officially recognizes your tax-exempt status.

Form: IRS Form 1023, Form 1023-EZ or Form 1024
Submit To: Internal Revenue Service (IRS)
How to File: Mail
Cost: $275 for Form 1023-EZ and $600 for Form 1023
Time Frame: Less than a month for Form 1023-EZ and 3-6 months for Form 1023

Step-11: State Tax Exemption

Once you have your IRS Determination Letter, you next need to figure out your state's requirements for tax-exempt status. This is another area that varies by state. You may also need to do periodic renewals for tax-exempt status.

In Kentucky, you obtain your state income tax exemption when you get your IRS Determination Letter.

For state sales tax exemption in Kentucky:

Form: 51A125: Application for Purchase Exemption
Submit To: Kentucky Department of Revenue
Cost: $0

Additional Notes:

- Include a copy of your articles of incorporation and IRS Determination Letter

Step-12: Charitable Solicitation Registration

This is yet another area where it varies between states, but most require it on an annual basis. This means you need to register with the state before fundraising from any resident of the state. Depending on the scope of your organization you may need to register in other states as well.

Overseen By: Kentucky Attorney General – Charities

Exemptions:
1. Religious organizations
2. Educational institutions
3. Membership organizations
4. PTAs and student groups

To file in Kentucky, you need to do the following:

Form: Include the following:
- Copy for most recent IRS 990
- Copy of IRS Determination Letter
- Copy of bylaws
- Copy of Articles of Incorporation

Submit To: Kansas Attorney General - Charities
How to File: Mail
Cost: $0
Step-13: Business Licenses and Permits

From here you will be all set to start your nonprofit. However, the work isn't over yet. You'll also need to stay in compliance with your nonprofit. Next, consider your required annual filings to remain legal.

Annual Renewal

1. IRS Renewals
    a. IRS Form 990
    b. Due the 15th day of the 5th month following the end of the taxable year.
2. Kentucky has no renewal requirements for corporate income tax exemption.
3. Kentucky has no renewal requirements for sales tax exemption.
4. Kentucky requires an annual report
    a. Filed with the Kentucky Secretary of State
    b. File the reminder postcard sent to you
    c. Filed by mail, in person or online
    d. Costs $15
    e. Due annually by June 30. Can be as early as January 1st.
    f. Your business will be dissolved or revoked if not filed within 60 days.
    g. The postcard must be signed by a member, partner or officer
    h. Can be filed online by anyone with authority
    i. The form doesn't need original signatures
5. Charitable Solicitation Renewal
    a. Filed with the Kentucky Attorney General - Charities
    b. Costs $0
    c. If URS is filed then it is due annually by December 31st. Otherwise due annually by 4 months and 15 days from fiscal year end.

LOUISIANA

Step-1: Name Your Nonprofit

The name of your nonprofit will establish its brand and will allow you to incorporate with the state. The name you choose cannot conflict with any other organization registered within the state of Louisiana. Make sure the name you choose is available and meets all state requirement. Search through the Louisiana Secretary of State - Commercial Division.

Step-2: Get Initial Directors and Incorporators

The incorporate is the individual who signs the Articles of Incorporation for your business. You will need at least one incorporator, but you can have additional. The directors are the governing body of your nonprofit and are stakeholders in the purpose and success of your nonprofit. You should have at least three directors who are unrelated individuals in order to meet IRS requirements. You'll also want to meet age and residency requirements.

Step-3: Selected a Registered Agent

The registered agent is responsible for receiving legal notices for your nonprofit. A registered agent needs to be physically living in the state and maintain an office open during regular business hours.

Step-4: Articles of Incorporation

The articles of incorporation are the official creation of your nonprofit. They show where and when the nonprofit was formed and provide the necessary information to verify the

nonprofits existence. Make sure your articles of incorporation meet state and IRS requirement.

Form: Articles of Incorporation - Louisiana Nonprofit
Submit To: Kentucky Secretary of State - Commercial Division
How to File: Mail, fax, in person or online
Cost: $75. Optional $30-50 expedite.
Time Frame: About 1 week. About 24 hours for $30 expedite. While you wait when filing in person with $50 expedite.

Additional Notes:
- When filing by mail includes the following:
    - Articles of Incorporation
    - Transmittal Information Cover Form
    - Registered Agent's Affidavit and Acknowledgement of Acceptance
    - Notarized Signature

Step-5: File with Recorder of Mortgages

After filing Articles of Incorporation, you have 30 days to file a copy of Articles of Incorporation certified by the Secretary of State and a Certificate of Incorporation with the office of the recorder of mortgages in the parish where your corporate headquarters will be.

Step-6: Get an Employer Identification Number (EIN)

This is a unique nine-digit number that the IRS assigned to identify your nonprofit. Your EIN is then used to open a bank account, apply for 501(c)(3) status and submit 990 IRS returns.

Form: IRS Form SS-4
Submit To: Internal Revenue Service (IRS)
How to File: Mail, phone, fax or online
Cost: $0
Time Frame: By phone or online is immediate, by fax is 4 days and by mail is 4-5 weeks.

Additional Notes:
- Print EIN before the closing session

Step-7: Storing Records

As you start a nonprofit, you will be faced with a number of official documents. Be sure you organize and store all of these records together for easy access later.

Step-8: Initial Governing Policies and Documents

The governing document for your nonprofit is your bylaws since they serve as the operating manual for your organization and need to be consistent with both the law and your articles of incorporation. The first meeting of your Board of Directors should be to review and ratify the bylaws.

You should also create and adopt a conflict of interest policy. This will guide you in what to do if someone in a key position within your nonprofit has competing interests and makes a decision that benefits themselves while harming your nonprofit. Organizational interests should be prioritized ahead of personal interests. All conflicts should be disclosed immediately.

Both the bylaws and the conflict of interest policy will need to be approved and adopted before applying to the IRS for 501(c)(3) status.

Step-9: Board of Directors Organizational Meeting

This initial meeting is the most productive and important one. You will approve bylaws, adopt the conflict of interest policy, elect directors, appoint officers and approve any resolutions like opening a bank account. Be sure to record the decisions made in meeting minutes.

Step-10: State Tax Identification Numbers and Accounts

Incorporating a nonprofit means, you will follow all state laws. Requirements vary by state so check with your individual state first.

In Louisiana there is a consolidated tax registration application:

Form: R-16019: Application for Louisiana Revenue Account Number
Submit To: Louisiana Department of Revenue
How to File: Mail or online
Cost: $0
Time Frame: About 3 days online. About 4-6 weeks by mail.

Step-11: File for 501(c) Status

This can seem like one of the most difficult steps in starting your nonprofit, but it also offers many benefits. After applying and submitting your documents, the IRS will give you a Determination Letter that officially recognizes your tax-exempt status.

Form: IRS Form 1023, Form 1023-EZ or Form 1024
Submit To: Internal Revenue Service (IRS)
How to File: Mail
Cost: $275 for Form 1023-EZ and $600 for Form 1023
Time Frame: Less than a month for Form 1023-EZ and 3-6 months for Form 1023
Step-12: State Tax Exemption

Once you have your IRS Determination Letter, you next need to figure out your state's requirements for tax-exempt status. This is another area that varies by state. You may also need to do periodic renewals for tax-exempt status.

For income tax exemption in Louisiana contact the Louisiana Department of Revenue and submit a copy of your IRS Determination Letter.

For state sales tax exemption in Louisiana:

Form: R-1048: Application for Exemption from Collection of Louisiana Sales Tax at Certain Fund-Raising Activities
Submit To: Kentucky Department of Revenue
Cost: $0

Step-13: Charitable Solicitation Registration

This is yet another area where it varies between states, but most require it on an annual basis. This means you need to register with the state before fundraising from any resident of the state. Depending on the scope of your organization you may need to register in other states as well.

Overseen By: Louisiana Department of Justice - Public Protection Division – Charities

Exemptions:
1. Religious organizations
2. Educational institutions
3. Hospitals and volunteer health organizations

To file in Louisiana, you need to do the following:

Form: Include the following:
- URS Multi-State Registration
- Copy of all contracts with professional solicitors
- Copy of recent IRS 990
- Copy of IRS Determination Letter
- Copy of Bylaws
- Copy of Articles of Incorporation
- List of other States where your nonprofit is registered

Submit To: Louisiana Department of Justice - Public Protection Division - Charities

How to File: Mail

Cost: $25

Additional Notes:
- Include all required attachments
- Include necessary signatures

Step-14: Business Licenses and Permits

From here you will be all set to start your nonprofit. However, the work isn't over yet. You'll also need to stay in compliance with your nonprofit. Next, consider your required annual filings to remain legal.

Annual Renewal

1. IRS Renewals
    a. IRS Form 990
    b. Due the 15th day of the 5th month following the end of the taxable year.
2. Louisiana has no renewal requirements for corporate income tax exemption.
3. Louisiana has no renewal requirements for sales tax exemption.
4. Louisiana requires an annual report

      a. Filed with the Louisiana Secretary of State - Commercial Division
      b. Filed by mail or online
      c. Costs $15
      d. Due annually by registration anniversary
      e. Your business will be dissolved or revoked if not filed in 3 years
      f. Can be filed by an officer, director, manager, member, partner or agent
      g. If filing by mail then original signatures are necessary

5. Charitable Solicitation Renewal
      a. Filed with the Louisiana Department of Justice - Public Protection Division - Charities
      b. Form URS Multi-State Registration
      c. Costs $25
      d. Filed by mail
      e. Due annually by the date of initial registration
      f. Include all attachments including IRS Form 990
      g. Include all required signatures

MAINE

Step-1: Name Your Nonprofit

The name of your nonprofit will establish its brand and will allow you to incorporate with the state. The name you choose cannot conflict with any other organization registered within the state of Maine. Make sure the name you choose is available and meets all state requirement. Search through the Maine Secretary of State - Bureau of Corporations, Elections, and Commissions.

Step-2: Get Initial Directors and Incorporators

The incorporate is the individual who signs the Articles of Incorporation for your business. You will need at least one incorporator, but you can have additional. The directors are the governing body of your nonprofit and are stakeholders in the purpose and success of your nonprofit. You should have at least three directors who are unrelated individuals in order to meet IRS requirements. You'll also want to meet age and residency requirements.

Step-3: Selected a Registered Agent

The registered agent is responsible for receiving legal notices for your nonprofit. A registered agent needs to be physically living in the state and maintain an office open during regular business hours.

Step-4: Articles of Incorporation

The articles of incorporation are the official creation of your nonprofit. They show where and when the nonprofit was formed and provide the necessary information to verify the

nonprofits existence. Make sure your articles of incorporation meet state and IRS requirement.

Form: MNPCA-6 (D): Articles of Incorporation
Submit To: Maine Secretary of State - Bureau of Corporations, Elections, and Commissions
How to File: Mail or in person
Cost: $40. Optional $50-100 expedite.
Time Frame: About 14 days. About 24 hours with $50 expedite. Immediate with $100 expedite.

Additional Notes:
- If filing by mail includes the filer on the contact cover form.
- Original signatures are required.

Step-5: Get an Employer Identification Number (EIN)

This is a unique nine-digit number that the IRS assigned to identify your nonprofit. Your EIN is then used to open a bank account, apply for 501(c)(3) status and submit 990 IRS returns.

Form: IRS Form SS-4
Submit To: Internal Revenue Service (IRS)
How to File: Mail, phone, fax or online
Cost: $0
Time Frame: By phone or online is immediate, by fax is 4 days and by mail is 4-5 weeks.

Additional Notes:
- Print EIN before the closing session

Step-6: Storing Records

As you start a nonprofit, you will be faced with a number of official documents. Be sure you organize and store all of these records together for easy access later.

Step-7: Initial Governing Policies and Documents

The governing document for your nonprofit is your bylaws since they serve as the operating manual for your organization and need to be consistent with both the law and your articles of incorporation. The first meeting of your Board of Directors should be to review and ratify the bylaws.

You should also create and adopt a conflict of interest policy. This will guide you in what to do if someone in a key position within your nonprofit has competing interests and makes a decision that benefits themselves while harming your nonprofit. Organizational interests should be prioritized ahead of personal interests. All conflicts should be disclosed immediately.

Both the bylaws and the conflict of interest policy will need to be approved and adopted before applying to the IRS for 501(c)(3) status.

Step-8: Board of Directors Organizational Meeting

This initial meeting is the most productive and important one. You will approve bylaws, adopt the conflict of interest policy, elect directors, appoint officers and approve any resolutions like opening a bank account. Be sure to record the decisions made in meeting minutes.

Step-9: State Tax Identification Numbers and Accounts

Incorporating a nonprofit means, you will follow all state laws. Requirements vary by state so check with your individual state first.

In Maine a single application is filed:

Form: Maine Application for Tax Registration
Submit To: Maine Revenue Services
How to File: Mail or online
Cost: $0

Step-10: File for 501(c) Status

This can seem like one of the most difficult steps in starting your nonprofit, but it also offers many benefits. After applying and submitting your documents, the IRS will give you a Determination Letter that officially recognizes your tax-exempt status.

Form: IRS Form 1023, Form 1023-EZ or Form 1024
Submit To: Internal Revenue Service (IRS)
How to File: Mail
Cost: $275 for Form 1023-EZ and $600 for Form 1023
Time Frame: Less than a month for Form 1023-EZ and 3-6 months for Form 1023

Step-11: State Tax Exemption

Once you have your IRS Determination Letter, you next need to figure out your state's requirements for tax-exempt status. This is another area that varies by state. You may also need to do periodic renewals for tax-exempt status.

For income tax exemption in Maine, you will receive it automatically with an IRS Determination Letter.

For state sales tax exemption in Maine contact the Maine Revenue Services.

Step-12: Charitable Solicitation Registration

This is yet another area where it varies between states, but most require it on an annual basis. This means you need to register with the state before fundraising from any resident of the state. Depending on the scope of your organization you may need to register in other states as well.

Overseen By: Maine Office of Professional and Occupation Registration.

Exemptions:
1. Solicitation of members
2. Appeal for individuals
3. Less than $35,000 contributions per the calendar year or less than 35 people contributing per calendar per year and no hired professional solicitors
4. Educational institutions
5. Hospitals
6. Free clinics

To file in Maine, you need to do the following:

Form: Include the following:
- Charitable Organization Application
- List of Directors/Officers
- List of individuals responsible for custody of contributions
- List of States your nonprofit is registered in for solicitation
- IRS Determination Letter
- Organization budget for the current fiscal year
- Contracts with professional solicitors

Submit To: Maine Office of Professional and Occupation Registration
How to File: Mail or online
Cost: $25 application + $25 license = $50 state fee

Additional Notes:
- Include all required attachments

Step-14: Business Licenses and Permits

From here you will be all set to start your nonprofit. However, the work isn't over yet. You'll also need to stay in compliance with your nonprofit. Next, consider your required annual filings to remain legal.

Annual Renewal

1. IRS Renewals
    a. IRS Form 990
    b. Due the 15th day of the 5th month following the end of the taxable year.
2. Maine has no renewal requirements for corporate income tax exemption.
3. Maine has no renewal requirements for sales tax exemption.
4. Maine requires an annual report
    a. Filed with the Maine Secretary of State - Bureau of Corporations, Elections, and Commissions
    b. Filed by mail or online
    c. Costs $35
    d. Due annually by June 1st
    e. $25 late fee
    f. May be filed by anyone with authority
    g. If filing by paper then original signatures are required
5. Charitable Solicitation Renewal

a. Filed with the Maine Office of Professional and Occupation Regulation
b. Form Charitable Organization Application and Annual Fundraising Activity Report for Charitable Organization
c. Costs $50
d. Filed by mail or online
e. Due annually by November 30th
f. Include all attachments
g. $50 late fee

MARYLAND

Step-1: Name Your Nonprofit

The name of your nonprofit will establish its brand and will allow you to incorporate with the state. The name you choose cannot conflict with any other organization registered within the state of Maryland. Make sure the name you choose is available and meets all state requirement. Search through the Maryland State Department of Assessments and Taxation.

Step-2: Choose a Nonprofit Structure

There are three types of nonprofit corporation structures to choose from in Maryland:
1. Religious Corporation
2. Tax-Exempt Nonstock Corporation for those filing for 501(c)(3) status
3. Nonstock Corporation

Step-3: Get Initial Directors and Incorporators

The incorporate is the individual who signs the Articles of Incorporation for your business. You will need at least one incorporator, but you can have additional. The directors are the governing body of your nonprofit and are stakeholders in the purpose and success of your nonprofit. You should have at least three directors who are unrelated individuals in order to meet IRS requirements. You'll also want to meet age and residency requirements.

Step-4: Selected a Registered Agent

The registered agent is responsible for receiving legal notices for your nonprofit. A registered agent needs to be physically living in the state and maintain an office open during regular business hours.

Step-5: Articles of Incorporation

The articles of incorporation are the official creation of your nonprofit. They show where and when the nonprofit was formed and provide the necessary information to verify the nonprofits existence. Make sure your articles of incorporation meet state and IRS requirement.

Form: Articles of Incorporation for Tax-exempt Nonstock Corporation
Submit To: Maryland State Department of Assessments and Taxation
How to File: Mail, fax, in person or online
Cost: $100 filing fee + $20 organization and capitalization fee + $50 development center fee when applying for 501(c)(3)(4) or optional $5 return mail fee + optional $50 expedite. Expedite fee is required when filing online, by fax or in person.
Time Frame: About 10 weeks. About 7 days with expediting fees. Same day if filed in person with appropriate expediting fees.

Step-6: Get an Employer Identification Number (EIN)

This is a unique nine-digit number that the IRS assigned to identify your nonprofit. Your EIN is then used to open a bank account, apply for 501(c)(3) status and submit 990 IRS returns.

Form: IRS Form SS-4
Submit To: Internal Revenue Service (IRS)
How to File: Mail, phone, fax or online
Cost: $0

Time Frame: By phone or online is immediate, by fax is 4 days and by mail is 4-5 weeks.

Additional Notes:
- Print EIN before the closing session

Step-7: Storing Records

As you start a nonprofit, you will be faced with a number of official documents. Be sure you organize and store all of these records together for easy access later.

Step-8: Initial Governing Policies and Documents

The governing document for your nonprofit is your bylaws since they serve as the operating manual for your organization and need to be consistent with both the law and your articles of incorporation. The first meeting of your Board of Directors should be to review and ratify the bylaws.

You should also create and adopt a conflict of interest policy. This will guide you in what to do if someone in a key position within your nonprofit has competing interests and makes a decision that benefits themselves while harming your nonprofit. Organizational interests should be prioritized ahead of personal interests. All conflicts should be disclosed immediately.

Both the bylaws and the conflict of interest policy will need to be approved and adopted before applying to the IRS for 501(c)(3) status.

Step-9: Board of Directors Organizational Meeting

This initial meeting is the most productive and important one. You will approve bylaws, adopt the conflict of interest policy, elect directors, appoint officers and approve any resolutions like opening a bank account. Be sure to record the decisions made in meeting minutes.

Step-10: State Tax Identification Numbers and Accounts

Incorporating a nonprofit means, you will follow all state laws. Requirements vary by state so check with your individual state first.

In Maryland apply with the following:

Form: CRA: Maryland Combined Registration Application
Submit To: Comptroller of Maryland
How to File: Mail or online
Cost: $0

Step-11: File for 501(c) Status

This can seem like one of the most difficult steps in starting your nonprofit, but it also offers many benefits. After applying and submitting your documents, the IRS will give you a Determination Letter that officially recognizes your tax-exempt status.

Form: IRS Form 1023, Form 1023-EZ or Form 1024
Submit To: Internal Revenue Service (IRS)
How to File: Mail
Cost: $275 for Form 1023-EZ and $600 for Form 1023
Time Frame: Less than a month for Form 1023-EZ and 3-6 months for Form 1023

Step-12: State Tax Exemption

Once you have your IRS Determination Letter, you next need to figure out your state's requirements for tax-exempt status. This is another area that varies by state. You may also need to do periodic renewals for tax-exempt status.

For income tax exemption in Maryland contact the Comptroller of Maryland.

For state sales tax exemption in Maryland contact the Comptroller of Maryland.

Step-13: Charitable Solicitation Registration

This is yet another area where it varies between states, but most require it on an annual basis. This means you need to register with the state before fundraising from any resident of the state. Depending on the scope of your organization you may need to register in other states as well.

Overseen By: Maryland Secretary of State - Charitable Organizations Division

Exemptions:
1. Religious organizations
2. Educational institutions
3. Membership organizations
4. Appeals for individuals
5. Grants
6. Volunteer firefighters

To file in Maryland, you need to do the following:

Form: URS or COR-92: Charity Registration
Submit To: Maryland Secretary of State - Charitable Organizations Division
How to File: Mail

Cost: $0-300 depending on contributions

Additional Notes:
- Include all required attachments
- Must be signed by the president, chairman or principal officer
- Signatures don't need to be notarized
- You will get a Certificate of Solicitation upon approval

Step-14: Business Licenses and Permits

From here you will be all set to start your nonprofit. However, the work isn't over yet. You'll also need to stay in compliance with your nonprofit. Next, consider your required annual filings to remain legal.

Annual Renewal

1. IRS Renewals
    a. IRS Form 990
    b. Due the 15th day of the 5th month following the end of the taxable year.
2. Maryland Corporate Tax Returns
    a. Filed with Comptroller of Maryland
    b. File Form 500
    c. Due three and a half months after the end of the fiscal year
3. Maryland Corporate Tax Exemption Renewal
    a. Filed with Comptroller of Maryland
    b. File Combined Registration Application
    c. Due every 5 years
4. Maryland Corporate Tax Exemption Renewal
    a. Filed with Comptroller of Maryland
    b. File Sales and Use Tax Exemption Certificate Renewal

  c. Due every 5 years
5. Maryland requires an annual report
  a. Filed with the Maryland State Department of Assessments and Taxation
  b. File Form 1 - Annual Report and Personal Property Tax Return
  c. Filed by mail or online
  d. Costs $0
  e. Due annually by April 15th
  f. Must be signed by principal or officer
  g. Must have original signatures
6. Charitable Solicitation Renewal
  a. Filed with the Maryland Secretary of State - Charitable Organizations Division
  b. Form Maryland Annual Update of Registration
  c. Costs $0-300 depending on contributions
  d. Filed by mail
  e. Due annually 6 months after close of the fiscal year
  f. Include all attachments, including an annual financial report

MASSACHUSETTS

Step-1: Name Your Nonprofit

The name of your nonprofit will establish its brand and will allow you to incorporate with the state. The name you choose cannot conflict with any other organization registered within the state of Massachusetts. Make sure the name you choose is available and meets all state requirement. Search through the Massachusetts Secretary of the Commonwealth

Step-2: Get Initial Directors and Incorporators

The incorporate is the individual who signs the Articles of Incorporation for your business. You will need at least one incorporator, but you can have additional. The directors are the governing body of your nonprofit and are stakeholders in the purpose and success of your nonprofit. You should have at least three directors who are unrelated individuals in order to meet IRS requirements. You'll also want to meet age and residency requirements.

Step-3: Selected a Registered Agent

The registered agent is responsible for receiving legal notices for your nonprofit. A registered agent needs to be physically living in the state and maintain an office open during regular business hours.

Step-4: Articles of Incorporation

The articles of incorporation are the official creation of your nonprofit. They show where and when the nonprofit was formed and provide the necessary information to verify the

nonprofits existence. Make sure your articles of incorporation meet state and IRS requirement.

Form: Articles of Organization
Submit To: Massachusetts Secretary of the Commonwealth
How to File: Mail, fax, in person or online
Cost: $35 by mail. $40 by fax or online.
Time Frame: About 2-3 days.

Step-5: Get an Employer Identification Number (EIN)

This is a unique nine-digit number that the IRS assigned to identify your nonprofit. Your EIN is then used to open a bank account, apply for 501(c)(3) status and submit 990 IRS returns.

Form: IRS Form SS-4
Submit To: Internal Revenue Service (IRS)
How to File: Mail, phone, fax or online
Cost: $0
Time Frame: By phone or online is immediate, by fax is 4 days and by mail is 4-5 weeks.

Additional Notes:
- Print EIN before the closing session

Step-6: Storing Records

As you start a nonprofit, you will be faced with a number of official documents. Be sure you organize and store all of these records together for easy access later.

Step-7: Initial Governing Policies and Documents

The governing document for your nonprofit is your bylaws since they serve as the operating manual for your organization and need to be consistent with both the law and your articles of incorporation. The first meeting of your Board of Directors should be to review and ratify the bylaws.

You should also create and adopt a conflict of interest policy. This will guide you in what to do if someone in a key position within your nonprofit has competing interests and makes a decision that benefits themselves while harming your nonprofit. Organizational interests should be prioritized ahead of personal interests. All conflicts should be disclosed immediately.

Both the bylaws and the conflict of interest policy will need to be approved and adopted before applying to the IRS for 501(c)(3) status.

Step-8: Board of Directors Organizational Meeting

This initial meeting is the most productive and important one. You will approve bylaws, adopt the conflict of interest policy, elect directors, appoint officers and approve any resolutions like opening a bank account. Be sure to record the decisions made in meeting minutes.

Step-9: State Tax Identification Numbers and Accounts

Incorporating a nonprofit means, you will follow all state laws. Requirements vary by state so check with your individual state first.

In Massachusetts offers a consolidated registration application:

Form: ST-1: Sales and Use Tax Registration
Submit To: Massachusetts Department of Revenue
How to File: Online

Step-10: File for 501(c) Status

This can seem like one of the most difficult steps in starting your nonprofit, but it also offers many benefits. After applying and submitting your documents, the IRS will give you a Determination Letter that officially recognizes your tax-exempt status.

Form: IRS Form 1023, Form 1023-EZ or Form 1024
Submit To: Internal Revenue Service (IRS)
How to File: Mail
Cost: $275 for Form 1023-EZ and $600 for Form 1023
Time Frame: Less than a month for Form 1023-EZ and 3-6 months for Form 1023

Step-11: State Tax Exemption

Once you have your IRS Determination Letter, you next need to figure out your state's requirements for tax-exempt status. This is another area that varies by state. You may also need to do periodic renewals for tax-exempt status.

For income tax exemption in Massachusetts:

- File with Massachusetts Department of Revenue
- Costs $0
- Submit the following:
    - Registration
    - Copy of IRS Determination Letter
    - Copy of Articles of Incorporation

For state sales tax exemption in Massachusetts contact the Massachusetts Department of Revenue.

Step-12: Charitable Solicitation Registration

This is yet another area where it varies between states, but most require it on an annual basis. This means you need to register with the state before fundraising from any resident of the state. Depending on the scope of your organization you may need to register in other states as well.

Overseen By: Massachusetts Attorney General - Non-Profit Organizations/Public Charities Division.

Exemptions:
1. Less than $5,000 in a fiscal year
2. Less than 10 contributors per year
3. Religious organizations
4. Fraternal organizations
5. Appeals for individuals

To file in Massachusetts, you need to do the following:

Form: PC
Submit To: Massachusetts Attorney General - Non-Profit Organizations/Public Charities Division
How to File: Mail
Cost: $100 Initial Fee + $50 for organizations registering before the end of the fiscal year and $32-2,000 depending on gross support and revenue.

Step-13: Business Licenses and Permits
From here you will be all set to start your nonprofit. However, the work isn't over yet. You'll also need to stay in compliance with your nonprofit. Next, consider your required annual filings to remain legal.

Annual Renewal

1. IRS Renewals
    a. IRS Form 990
    b. Due the 15th day of the 5th month following the end of the taxable year.
2. Massachusetts has no corporate tax exemption renewal requirements.
3. Massachusetts has no sales tax exemption renewal requirements.
4. Massachusetts requires an annual report
    a. Filed with the Massachusetts Secretary of the Commonwealth
    b. File the Annual Report
    c. Filed by mail, in person or online
    d. Costs $15 for mail. $18.50 online.
    e. Due annually by November 1st
    f. May be filed by anyone with authority
    g. Does not need original signatures
5. Charitable Solicitation Renewal
    a. Filed with the Massachusetts Attorney General - Non-Profit Organizations/Public Charities Division
    b. Form PC
    c. Costs $35-2,000 depending on gross revenue and support
    d. Filed by mail
    e. Due annually four and a half months after the close of the fiscal year
    f. Attach a copy of IRS Form 990
    g. Charities raising over $200,000 need to include a financial statement

MICHIGAN

Step-1: Name Your Nonprofit

The name of your nonprofit will establish its brand and will allow you to incorporate with the state. The name you choose cannot conflict with any other organization registered within the state of Michigan. Make sure the name you choose is available and meets all state requirement. Search through the Michigan Department of Licensing and Regulatory Affairs - Corporations Division.

Step-2: Get Initial Directors and Incorporators

The incorporate is the individual who signs the Articles of Incorporation for your business. You will need at least one incorporator, but you can have additional. The directors are the governing body of your nonprofit and are stakeholders in the purpose and success of your nonprofit. You should have at least three directors who are unrelated individuals in order to meet IRS requirements. You'll also want to meet age and residency requirements.

Step-3: Selected a Registered Agent

The registered agent is responsible for receiving legal notices for your nonprofit. A registered agent needs to be physically living in the state and maintain an office open during regular business hours.

Step-4: Articles of Incorporation

The articles of incorporation are the official creation of your nonprofit. They show where and when the nonprofit was formed and provide the necessary information to verify the

nonprofits existence. Make sure your articles of incorporation meet state and IRS requirement.

Form: Articles of Incorporation - Nonprofit
Submit To: Michigan Department of Licensing and Regulatory Affairs - Corporations Division
How to File: Mail or in person
Cost: $20. Optional $50-1,000 expedite.
Time Frame: About 5-7 days and documents returned in about 4 weeks. About 24 hours for $50. Same day for $100. 2 hours for $100. 1 hour for $1,000.

Additional Notes:
- You only need to submit one original document

Step-5: Get an Employer Identification Number (EIN)

This is a unique nine-digit number that the IRS assigned to identify your nonprofit. Your EIN is then used to open a bank account, apply for 501(c)(3) status and submit 990 IRS returns.

Form: IRS Form SS-4
Submit To: Internal Revenue Service (IRS)
How to File: Mail, phone, fax or online
Cost: $0
Time Frame: By phone or online is immediate, by fax is 4 days and by mail is 4-5 weeks.

Additional Notes:
- Print EIN before the closing session

Step-6: Storing Records

As you start a nonprofit, you will be faced with a number of official documents. Be sure you organize and store all of these records together for easy access later.

Step-7: Initial Governing Policies and Documents

The governing document for your nonprofit is your bylaws since they serve as the operating manual for your organization and need to be consistent with both the law and your articles of incorporation. The first meeting of your Board of Directors should be to review and ratify the bylaws.

You should also create and adopt a conflict of interest policy. This will guide you in what to do if someone in a key position within your nonprofit has competing interests and makes a decision that benefits themselves while harming your nonprofit. Organizational interests should be prioritized ahead of personal interests. All conflicts should be disclosed immediately.

Both the bylaws and the conflict of interest policy will need to be approved and adopted before applying to the IRS for 501(c)(3) status.

Step-8: Board of Directors Organizational Meeting

This initial meeting is the most productive and important one. You will approve bylaws, adopt the conflict of interest policy, elect directors, appoint officers and approve any resolutions like opening a bank account. Be sure to record the decisions made in meeting minutes.

Step-9: State Tax Identification Numbers and Accounts

Incorporating a nonprofit means, you will follow all state laws. Requirements vary by state so check with your individual state first.

In Michigan you can register through the following:

Form: 518: Registration for Business Taxes
Submit To: Michigan Department of Treasury
How to File: Mail, fax or online
Cost: $0
Time Frame: About 6 weeks

Step-10: File for 501(c) Status

This can seem like one of the most difficult steps in starting your nonprofit, but it also offers many benefits. After applying and submitting your documents, the IRS will give you a Determination Letter that officially recognizes your tax-exempt status.

Form: IRS Form 1023, Form 1023-EZ or Form 1024
Submit To: Internal Revenue Service (IRS)
How to File: Mail
Cost: $275 for Form 1023-EZ and $600 for Form 1023
Time Frame: Less than a month for Form 1023-EZ and 3-6 months for Form 1023

Step-11: State Tax Exemption

Once you have your IRS Determination Letter, you next need to figure out your state's requirements for tax-exempt status. This is another area that varies by state. You may also need to do periodic renewals for tax-exempt status.

You don't need to file for income tax exemption in Michigan

You don't need to file for sales tax exemption in Michigan

Step-12: Charitable Solicitation Registration

This is yet another area where it varies between states, but most require it on an annual basis. This means you need to register with the state before fundraising from any resident of the state. Depending on the scope of your organization you may need to register in other states as well.

Overseen By: Michigan Attorney General - Charitable Trust Section

Exemptions:
1. Less than $25,000 in a 12 month period
2. Religious organizations
3. Educational institutions
4. Appeals for individuals
5. Veterans organizations
6. PTAs
7. Advocacy/Lobbying organizations
8. Child-care providers
9. Service clubs

To file in Michigan you need to do the following:

Form: URS with Supplement or CTS-01: Initial Solicitation Registration Form
Submit To: Michigan Attorney General - Charitable Trust Section
How to File: Mail or online
Cost: $0
Additional Notes:
- Must be signed by one principal officer or director
- Signatures don't need to be notarized

Step-13: Business Licenses and Permits

From here you will be all set to start your nonprofit. However, the work isn't over yet. You'll also need to stay in compliance with your nonprofit. Next, consider your required annual filings to remain legal.

Annual Renewal
1. IRS Renewals
    a. IRS Form 990
    b. Due the 15th day of the 5th month following the end of the taxable year.
2. Michigan has no corporate tax exemption renewal requirements.
3. Michigan has no sales tax exemption renewal requirements.
4. Michigan requires an annual report
    a. Filed with the Michigan Department of Licensing and Regulatory Affairs - Corporations Division
    b. File, the Annual Report, sent to you
    c. Filed by mail, in person or online
    d. Costs $20
    e. Due annually by October 1st
    f. The corporation is dissolved if no filing is done in 2 years
    g. May be filed by anyone with authority
    h. Does not need original signatures
5. Charitable Solicitation Renewal
    a. Filed with the Michigan Attorney General - Charitable Trust Section
    b. Form URS with Supplement or CTS-02: Renewal Solicitation Registration Form
    c. Costs $0
    d. Filed by mail or online
    e. Due annually seven months after the close of the fiscal year

MINNESOTA

Step-1: Name Your Nonprofit

The name of your nonprofit will establish its brand and will allow you to incorporate with the state. The name you choose cannot conflict with any other organization registered within the state of Minnesota. Make sure the name you choose is available and meets all state requirement. Search through the Minnesota Secretary of State.

Step-2: Get Initial Directors and Incorporators

The incorporate is the individual who signs the Articles of Incorporation for your business. You will need at least one incorporator, but you can have additional. The directors are the governing body of your nonprofit and are stakeholders in the purpose and success of your nonprofit. You should have at least three directors who are unrelated individuals in order to meet IRS requirements. You'll also want to meet age and residency requirements.

Step-3: Selected a Registered Agent

The registered agent is responsible for receiving legal notices for your nonprofit. A registered agent needs to be physically living in the state and maintain an office open during regular business hours.

Step-4: Articles of Incorporation

The articles of incorporation are the official creation of your nonprofit. They show where and when the nonprofit was formed and provide the necessary information to verify the nonprofits existence. Make sure your articles of incorporation meet state and IRS requirement.

Form: Articles of Incorporation - Original Filing
Submit To: Minnesota Secretary of State
How to File: Mail, in person or online
Cost: $70 by mail. $90 online or in person expedite.
Time Frame: About 5-7 days by mail. About 24 hours online.

Additional Notes:
- Keep the original signed copy for your records and submit a copy.

Step-5: Get an Employer Identification Number (EIN)

This is a unique nine-digit number that the IRS assigned to identify your nonprofit. Your EIN is then used to open a bank account, apply for 501(c)(3) status and submit 990 IRS returns.

Form: IRS Form SS-4
Submit To: Internal Revenue Service (IRS)
How to File: Mail, phone, fax or online
Cost: $0
Time Frame: By phone or online is immediate, by fax is 4 days and by mail is 4-5 weeks.

Additional Notes:
- Print EIN before the closing session

Step-6: Storing Records

As you start a nonprofit, you will be faced with a number of official documents. Be sure you organize and store all of these records together for easy access later.

Step-7: Initial Governing Policies and Documents

The governing document for your nonprofit is your bylaws since they serve as the operating manual for your organization and need to be consistent with both the law and your articles of incorporation. The first meeting of your Board of Directors should be to review and ratify the bylaws.

You should also create and adopt a conflict of interest policy. This will guide you in what to do if someone in a key position within your nonprofit has competing interests and makes a decision that benefits themselves while harming your nonprofit. Organizational interests should be prioritized ahead of personal interests. All conflicts should be disclosed immediately.

Both the bylaws and the conflict of interest policy will need to be approved and adopted before applying to the IRS for 501(c)(3) status.

Step-8: Board of Directors Organizational Meeting

This initial meeting is the most productive and important one. You will approve bylaws, adopt the conflict of interest policy, elect directors, appoint officers and approve any resolutions like opening a bank account. Be sure to record the decisions made in meeting minutes.

Step-9: State Tax Identification Numbers and Accounts

Incorporating a nonprofit means, you will follow all state laws. Requirements vary by state so check with your individual state first.
In Minnesota you can register through the following:

Form: ABR: Minnesota Revenue Application for Business Registration
Submit To: Minnesota Department of Revenue
How to File: Mail, fax, phone or online

Cost: $0

Step-10: File for 501(c) Status

This can seem like one of the most difficult steps in starting your nonprofit, but it also offers many benefits. After applying and submitting your documents, the IRS will give you a Determination Letter that officially recognizes your tax-exempt status.

Form: IRS Form 1023, Form 1023-EZ or Form 1024
Submit To: Internal Revenue Service (IRS)
How to File: Mail
Cost: $275 for Form 1023-EZ and $600 for Form 1023
Time Frame: Less than a month for Form 1023-EZ and 3-6 months for Form 1023

Step-11: State Tax Exemption

Once you have your IRS Determination Letter, you next need to figure out your state's requirements for tax-exempt status. This is another area that varies by state. You may also need to do periodic renewals for tax-exempt status.

You don't need to file for income tax exemption in Minnesota

To file for sales tax exemption in Minnesota:

Form: ST16: Application for Exempt Status
Submit To: Minnesota Department of Revenue
Cost: $0

Step-12: Charitable Solicitation Registration

This is yet another area where it varies between states, but most require it on an annual basis. This means you need to register with the state before fundraising from any resident of the state. Depending on the scope of your organization you may need to register in other states as well.

Overseen By: Minnesota Attorney General – Charities

Exemptions:
1. Less than $25,000 in a fiscal year
2. Religious organizations
3. Educational institutions
4. Appeals for individuals
5. Membership organizations
6. Private foundations

To file in Minnesota, you need to do the following:

Form: URS with Supplement or Charitable Organization Initial Registration and Annual Report Form
Submit To: Minnesota Attorney General - Charities
How to File: Mail or online
Cost: $25

Additional Notes:
- Attach all necessary documents; larger corporations will need a financial statement
- Must be signed by two officers
- Signatures don't need to be notarized

Step-13: Business Licenses and Permits

From here you will be all set to start your nonprofit. However, the work isn't over yet. You'll also need to stay in compliance with your nonprofit. Next, consider your required annual filings to remain legal.

Annual Renewal

1. IRS Renewals
    a. IRS Form 990
    b. Due the 15th day of the 5th month following the end of the taxable year.
2. For Minnesota Corporate Tax Returns
    a. File M4NP
    b. File with Minnesota Department of Revenue
    c. Due four and a half months after fiscal year end
3. Minnesota has no corporate tax exemption renewal requirements.
4. Minnesota has no sales tax exemption renewal requirements.
5. Minnesota requires an annual report
    a. Filed with the Minnesota Secretary of State
    b. File the Annual Renewal
    c. Filed by mail, in person or online
    d. Costs $0
    e. Due annually by December 31st
    f. Dissolution or revocation if not filed by January 1st
    g. May be filed by anyone with authority
    h. Does not need original signatures
6. Charitable Solicitation Renewal
    a. Filed with the Minnesota Attorney General - Charities
    b. Form URS with Supplement or Charitable Organization Initial Registration and Annual Report Form
    c. Costs $25
    d. Filed by mail or online

e. Due annually six and a half months after the close of the fiscal year
f. Attach all necessary documents include IRS Form 990 and financial statements for larger corporations

MISSISSIPPI

Step-1: Name Your Nonprofit

The name of your nonprofit will establish its brand and will allow you to incorporate with the state. The name you choose cannot conflict with any other organization registered within the state of Mississippi. Make sure the name you choose is available and meets all state requirement. Search through the Mississippi Secretary of State.

Step-2: Get Initial Directors and Incorporators

The incorporate is the individual who signs the Articles of Incorporation for your business. You will need at least one incorporator, but you can have additional. The directors are the governing body of your nonprofit and are stakeholders in the purpose and success of your nonprofit. You should have at least three directors who are unrelated individuals in order to meet IRS requirements. You'll also want to meet age and residency requirements.

Step-3: Selected a Registered Agent

The registered agent is responsible for receiving legal notices for your nonprofit. A registered agent needs to be physically living in the state and maintain an office open during regular business hours.

Step-4: Articles of Incorporation

The articles of incorporation are the official creation of your nonprofit. They show where and when the nonprofit was formed and provide the necessary information to verify the nonprofits existence. Make sure your articles of incorporation meet state and IRS requirement.

Form: Articles of Incorporation
Submit To: Mississippi Secretary of State
How to File: Online
Cost: $50
Time Frame: About 2-3 days

Step-5: Get an Employer Identification Number (EIN)

This is a unique nine-digit number that the IRS assigned to identify your nonprofit. Your EIN is then used to open a bank account, apply for 501(c)(3) status and submit 990 IRS returns.

Form: IRS Form SS-4
Submit To: Internal Revenue Service (IRS)
How to File: Mail, phone, fax or online
Cost: $0
Time Frame: By phone or online is immediate, by fax is 4 days and by mail is 4-5 weeks.

Additional Notes:
- Print EIN before the closing session

Step-6: Storing Records

As you start a nonprofit, you will be faced with a number of official documents. Be sure you organize and store all of these records together for easy access later.

Step-7: Initial Governing Policies and Documents

The governing document for your nonprofit is your bylaws since they serve as the operating manual for your organization and need to be consistent with both the law and

your articles of incorporation. The first meeting of your Board of Directors should be to review and ratify the bylaws.

You should also create and adopt a conflict of interest policy. This will guide you in what to do if someone in a key position within your nonprofit has competing interests and makes a decision that benefits themselves while harming your nonprofit. Organizational interests should be prioritized ahead of personal interests. All conflicts should be disclosed immediately.

Both the bylaws and the conflict of interest policy will need to be approved and adopted before applying to the IRS for 501(c)(3) status.

Step-8: Board of Directors Organizational Meeting

This initial meeting is the most productive and important one. You will approve bylaws, adopt the conflict of interest policy, elect directors, appoint officers and approve any resolutions like opening a bank account. Be sure to record the decisions made in meeting minutes.

Step-9: State Tax Identification Numbers and Accounts

Incorporating a nonprofit means, you will follow all state laws. Requirements vary by state so check with your individual state first.

In Mississippi you can register through the following:

Form: Mississippi Taxpayer Access Point
Submit To: Mississippi Department of Revenue
How to File: Online
Cost: $0

Additional Notes:
- You'll need an EIN and Business ID from the Secretary of State before filing

Step-10: File for 501(c) Status

This can seem like one of the most difficult steps in starting your nonprofit, but it also offers many benefits. After applying and submitting your documents, the IRS will give you a Determination Letter that officially recognizes your tax-exempt status.

Form: IRS Form 1023, Form 1023-EZ or Form 1024
Submit To: Internal Revenue Service (IRS)
How to File: Mail
Cost: $275 for Form 1023-EZ and $600 for Form 1023
Time Frame: Less than a month for Form 1023-EZ and 3-6 months for Form 1023

Step-11: State Tax Exemption

Once you have your IRS Determination Letter, you next need to figure out your state's requirements for tax-exempt status. This is another area that varies by state. You may also need to do periodic renewals for tax-exempt status.

For income tax exemption in Mississippi contact the Mississippi Department of Revenue

Mississippi nonprofits aren't exempt from sales tax.

Step-12: Charitable Solicitation Registration

This is yet another area where it varies between states, but most require it on an annual basis. This means you need to register with the state before fundraising from any

resident of the state. Depending on the scope of your organization you may need to register in other states as well.

Overseen By: Mississippi Secretary of State - Charities Division

Exemptions:
1. Less than $25,000 in a 12 month period ending June 30
2. Religious organizations
3. Educational institutions
4. Appeals for individuals
5. Membership organizations
6. Humane societies

To file in Mississippi, you need to do the following:

Submit To: Mississippi Secretary of State - Charities Division
How to File: Online
Cost: $50

Additional Notes:
- Attach all necessary documents; larger corporations will need a financial statement
- Must be signed by the CFO and president
- Signatures must be notarized
- Certificate of Registration is issued upon approval

Step-13: Business Licenses and Permits

From here you will be all set to start your nonprofit. However, the work isn't over yet. You'll also need to stay in compliance with your nonprofit. Next, consider your required annual filings to remain legal.

Annual Renewal

1. IRS Renewals
    a. IRS Form 990
    b. Due the 15th day of the 5th month following the end of the taxable year.
2. Mississippi has no corporate tax exemption renewal requirements.
3. Mississippi has no sales tax exemption renewal requirements.
4. Mississippi requires a status report
    a. Filed with the Mississippi Secretary of State
    b. File Form F0088
    c. Filed online
    d. Costs $25
    e. Due within 90 days of the request and can be requested every 5 years
5. Charitable Solicitation Renewal
    a. Filed with the Mississippi Secretary of State - Charities Division
    b. Costs $50
    c. Filed online
    d. Due annually 4 months and 15 days after fiscal year end
    e. Attach all necessary documents include IRS Form 990 and financial statements for larger corporations

MISSOURI

Step-1: Name Your Nonprofit

The name of your nonprofit will establish its brand and will allow you to incorporate with the state. The name you choose cannot conflict with any other organization registered within the state of Missouri. Make sure the name you choose is available and meets all state requirement. Search through the Missouri Secretary of State - Corporations Division.

Step-2: Get Initial Directors and Incorporators

The incorporate is the individual who signs the Articles of Incorporation for your business. You will need at least one incorporator, but you can have additional. The directors are the governing body of your nonprofit and are stakeholders in the purpose and success of your nonprofit. You should have at least three directors who are unrelated individuals in order to meet IRS requirements. You'll also want to meet age and residency requirements.

Step-3: Selected a Registered Agent

The registered agent is responsible for receiving legal notices for your nonprofit. A registered agent needs to be physically living in the state and maintain an office open during regular business hours.

Step-4: Articles of Incorporation

The articles of incorporation are the official creation of your nonprofit. They show where and when the nonprofit was formed and provide the necessary information to verify the

nonprofits existence. Make sure your articles of incorporation meet state and IRS requirement.

Form: Articles of Incorporation of a Nonprofit Corporation and Domestic Nonprofit Instruction Sheet
Submit To: Missouri Secretary of State - Corporations Division
How to File: Mail or fax
Cost: $25
Time Frame: About 4-7 days by mail. About 1-3 days by fax

Additional Notes:
- Need to submit original signatures

Step-5: Get an Employer Identification Number (EIN)

This is a unique nine-digit number that the IRS assigned to identify your nonprofit. Your EIN is then used to open a bank account, apply for 501(c)(3) status and submit 990 IRS returns.

Form: IRS Form SS-4
Submit To: Internal Revenue Service (IRS)
How to File: Mail, phone, fax or online
Cost: $0
Time Frame: By phone or online is immediate, by fax is 4 days and by mail is 4-5 weeks.

Additional Notes:
- Print EIN before the closing session

Step-6: Storing Records

As you start a nonprofit, you will be faced with a number of official documents. Be sure you organize and store all of these records together for easy access later.

Step-7: Initial Governing Policies and Documents

The governing document for your nonprofit is your bylaws since they serve as the operating manual for your organization and need to be consistent with both the law and your articles of incorporation. The first meeting of your Board of Directors should be to review and ratify the bylaws.

You should also create and adopt a conflict of interest policy. This will guide you in what to do if someone in a key position within your nonprofit has competing interests and makes a decision that benefits themselves while harming your nonprofit. Organizational interests should be prioritized ahead of personal interests. All conflicts should be disclosed immediately.

Both the bylaws and the conflict of interest policy will need to be approved and adopted before applying to the IRS for 501(c)(3) status.

Step-8: Board of Directors Organizational Meeting
This initial meeting is the most productive and important one. You will approve bylaws, adopt the conflict of interest policy, elect directors, appoint officers and approve any resolutions like opening a bank account. Be sure to record the decisions made in meeting minutes.

Step-9: State Tax Identification Numbers and Accounts

Incorporating a nonprofit means, you will follow all state laws. Requirements vary by state so check with your individual state first.

In Missouri you can register through the following:

Form: Missouri Online Business Registration System or Form 2643: Missouri Tax Registration Application
Submit To: Missouri Department of Revenue
How to File: Mail or online
Cost: $0

Additional Notes:
- You'll need an EIN before registering

Step-10: File for 501(c) Status

This can seem like one of the most difficult steps in starting your nonprofit, but it also offers many benefits. After applying and submitting your documents, the IRS will give you a Determination Letter that officially recognizes your tax-exempt status.

Form: IRS Form 1023, Form 1023-EZ or Form 1024
Submit To: Internal Revenue Service (IRS)
How to File: Mail
Cost: $275 for Form 1023-EZ and $600 for Form 1023
Time Frame: Less than a month for Form 1023-EZ and 3-6 months for Form 1023

Step-11: State Tax Exemption

Once you have your IRS Determination Letter, you next need to figure out your state's requirements for tax-exempt status. This is another area that varies by state. You may also need to do periodic renewals for tax-exempt status.

You don't need to file for corporate tax exemption in Missouri.

For sales tax exemption in Missouri:

Form: 1746: Missouri Sales or Use Tax Exemption Application
Submit To: Missouri Department of Revenue
Cost: $0

Step-12: Charitable Solicitation Registration

This is yet another area where it varies between states, but most require it on an annual basis. This means you need to register with the state before fundraising from any resident of the state. Depending on the scope of your organization you may need to register in other states as well.

Overseen By: Missouri Attorney General - Charities

To file in Missouri, you need to do the following:

Form: Initial Registration Statement
Submit To: Missouri Attorney General - Charities
How to File: Mail
Cost: $15

Additional Notes:
- Attach all necessary documents
- Needs one authorized signature
- Needs to be notarized

Step-13: Business Licenses and Permits

From here you will be all set to start your nonprofit. However, the work isn't over yet. You'll also need to stay in compliance with your nonprofit. Next, consider your required annual filings to remain legal.

Annual Renewal

1. IRS Renewals
    a. IRS Form 990
    b. Due the 15th day of the 5th month following the end of the taxable year.
2. Missouri has no corporate tax exemption renewal requirements.
3. Missouri has no sales tax exemption renewal requirements.
4. Missouri requires a registration report
    a. Filed with the Missouri Secretary of State - Corporations Division
    b. Filed by mail or online
    c. Costs $15 by mail or $10 online
    d. Due annually by August 31st
    e. $15 late fee
5. Charitable Solicitation Renewal
    a. Filed with the Missouri Attorney General - Charities
    b. File Charitable Organization Annual Report Form
    c. Costs $15
    d. Filed by mail
    e. Due annually within 75 days of the end of the fiscal year

MONTANA

Step-1: Name Your Nonprofit

The name of your nonprofit will establish its brand and will allow you to incorporate with the state. The name you choose cannot conflict with any other organization registered within the state of Montana. Make sure the name you choose is available and meets all state requirement. Search through the Montana Secretary of State.

Step-2: Get Initial Directors and Incorporators

The incorporate is the individual who signs the Articles of Incorporation for your business. You will need at least one incorporator, but you can have additional. The directors are the governing body of your nonprofit and are stakeholders in the purpose and success of your nonprofit. You should have at least three directors who are unrelated individuals in order to meet IRS requirements. You'll also want to meet age and residency requirements.

Step-3: Selected a Registered Agent

The registered agent is responsible for receiving legal notices for your nonprofit. A registered agent needs to be physically living in the state and maintain an office open during regular business hours.

Step-4: Articles of Incorporation

The articles of incorporation are the official creation of your nonprofit. They show where and when the nonprofit was formed and provide the necessary information to verify the nonprofits existence. Make sure your articles of incorporation meet state and IRS requirement.

Form: Articles of Incorporation
Submit To: Montana Secretary of State
How to File: Online
Cost: $20
Time Frame: About 10 days. Expedited available.

Additional Notes:
- Need to submit original documents

Step-5: Get an Employer Identification Number (EIN)

This is a unique nine-digit number that the IRS assigned to identify your nonprofit. Your EIN is then used to open a bank account, apply for 501(c)(3) status and submit 990 IRS returns.

Form: IRS Form SS-4
Submit To: Internal Revenue Service (IRS)
How to File: Mail, phone, fax or online
Cost: $0
Time Frame: By phone or online is immediate, by fax is 4 days and by mail is 4-5 weeks.

Additional Notes:
- Print EIN before the closing session

Step-6: Storing Records

As you start a nonprofit, you will be faced with a number of official documents. Be sure you organize and store all of these records together for easy access later.

Step-7: Initial Governing Policies and Documents

The governing document for your nonprofit is your bylaws since they serve as the operating manual for your organization and need to be consistent with both the law and your articles of incorporation. The first meeting of your Board of Directors should be to review and ratify the bylaws.

You should also create and adopt a conflict of interest policy. This will guide you in what to do if someone in a key position within your nonprofit has competing interests and makes a decision that benefits themselves while harming your nonprofit. Organizational interests should be prioritized ahead of personal interests. All conflicts should be disclosed immediately.

Both the bylaws and the conflict of interest policy will need to be approved and adopted before applying to the IRS for 501(c)(3) status.

Step-8: Board of Directors Organizational Meeting

This initial meeting is the most productive and important one. You will approve bylaws, adopt the conflict of interest policy, elect directors, appoint officers and approve any resolutions like opening a bank account. Be sure to record the decisions made in meeting minutes.

Step-9: State Tax Identification Numbers and Accounts

Incorporating a nonprofit means, you will follow all state laws. Requirements vary by state so check with your individual state first.

In Montana, you can contact the Montana Department of Revenue to apply.

Step-10: File for 501(c) Status

This can seem like one of the most difficult steps in starting your nonprofit, but it also offers many benefits. After applying and submitting your documents, the IRS will give you a Determination Letter that officially recognizes your tax-exempt status.

Form: IRS Form 1023, Form 1023-EZ or Form 1024
Submit To: Internal Revenue Service (IRS)
How to File: Mail
Cost: $275 for Form 1023-EZ and $600 for Form 1023
Time Frame: Less than a month for Form 1023-EZ and 3-6 months for Form 1023

Step-11: State Tax Exemption

Once you have your IRS Determination Letter, you next need to figure out your state's requirements for tax-exempt status. This is another area that varies by state. You may also need to do periodic renewals for tax-exempt status.

For income tax exemption in Montana:

Form: Montana Tax-Exempt Status Request Form
Submit To: Montana Department of Revenue
Cost: $0

Montana doesn't have a sales tax.

Step-12: Charitable Solicitation Registration

This is yet another area where it varies between states, but most require it on an annual basis. This means you need to register with the state before fundraising from any resident of the state. Depending on the scope of your organization you may need to register in other states as well.

Montana doesn't require this registration. However, some counties and municipalities may require registration.

Step-13: Business Licenses and Permits

From here you will be all set to start your nonprofit. However, the work isn't over yet. You'll also need to stay in compliance with your nonprofit. Next, consider your required annual filings to remain legal.

Annual Renewal

1. IRS Renewals
    a. IRS Form 990
    b. Due the 15th day of the 5th month following the end of the taxable year.
2. Montana has no corporate tax exemption renewal requirements.
3. Montana has no sales tax exemption renewal requirements.
4. Montana requires an annual report
    a. Filed with the Montana Secretary of State
    b. Filed online
    c. Costs $20
    d. Due annually by April 15th
    e. $15 late fee
    f. Filed by anyone with authority
    g. Does not need original signatures
    h. Provide an email address to receive an approval confirmation

NEBRASKA

Step-1: Name Your Nonprofit

The name of your nonprofit will establish its brand and will allow you to incorporate with the state. The name you choose cannot conflict with any other organization registered within the state of Nebraska. Make sure the name you choose is available and meets all state requirement. Search through the Nebraska Secretary of State.

Step-2: Get Initial Directors and Incorporators

The incorporate is the individual who signs the Articles of Incorporation for your business. You will need at least one incorporator, but you can have additional. The directors are the governing body of your nonprofit and are stakeholders in the purpose and success of your nonprofit. You should have at least three directors who are unrelated individuals in order to meet IRS requirements. You'll also want to meet age and residency requirements.

Step-3: Selected a Registered Agent

The registered agent is responsible for receiving legal notices for your nonprofit. A registered agent needs to be physically living in the state and maintain an office open during regular business hours.

Step-4: Articles of Incorporation

The articles of incorporation are the official creation of your nonprofit. They show where and when the nonprofit was formed and provide the necessary information to verify the nonprofits existence. Make sure your articles of incorporation meet state and IRS requirement.

Form: Articles of Incorporation
Submit To: Nebraska Secretary of State
How to File: Mail, in person or online
Cost: $10 + $5/page recording fee
Time Frame: About 1-2 days online. About 5-7 days by mail.

Additional Notes:
- Submit two copies

Step-5: Get an Employer Identification Number (EIN)

This is a unique nine-digit number that the IRS assigned to identify your nonprofit. Your EIN is then used to open a bank account, apply for 501(c)(3) status and submit 990 IRS returns.

Form: IRS Form SS-4
Submit To: Internal Revenue Service (IRS)
How to File: Mail, phone, fax or online
Cost: $0
Time Frame: By phone or online is immediate, by fax is 4 days and by mail is 4-5 weeks.

Additional Notes:
- Print EIN before the closing session

Step-6: Storing Records

As you start a nonprofit, you will be faced with a number of official documents. Be sure you organize and store all of these records together for easy access later.

Step-7: Initial Governing Policies and Documents

The governing document for your nonprofit is your bylaws since they serve as the operating manual for your organization and need to be consistent with both the law and your articles of incorporation. The first meeting of your Board of Directors should be to review and ratify the bylaws.

You should also create and adopt a conflict of interest policy. This will guide you in what to do if someone in a key position within your nonprofit has competing interests and makes a decision that benefits themselves while harming your nonprofit. Organizational interests should be prioritized ahead of personal interests. All conflicts should be disclosed immediately.

Both the bylaws and the conflict of interest policy will need to be approved and adopted before applying to the IRS for 501(c)(3) status.

Step-8: Board of Directors Organizational Meeting

This initial meeting is the most productive and important one. You will approve bylaws, adopt the conflict of interest policy, elect directors, appoint officers and approve any resolutions like opening a bank account. Be sure to record the decisions made in meeting minutes.

Step-9: State Tax Identification Numbers and Accounts

Incorporating a nonprofit means, you will follow all state laws. Requirements vary by state so check with your individual state first.
To apply in Nebraska:

Form: 20: Nebraska Tax Application
Submit To: Nebraska Department of Revenue
How to File: Mail

Cost: $0

Time Frame: About 2 weeks

Step-10: File for 501(c) Status

This can seem like one of the most difficult steps in starting your nonprofit, but it also offers many benefits. After applying and submitting your documents, the IRS will give you a Determination Letter that officially recognizes your tax-exempt status.

Form: IRS Form 1023, Form 1023-EZ or Form 1024
Submit To: Internal Revenue Service (IRS)
How to File: Mail
Cost: $275 for Form 1023-EZ and $600 for Form 1023
Time Frame: Less than a month for Form 1023-EZ and 3-6 months for Form 1023

Step-11: State Tax Exemption

Once you have your IRS Determination Letter, you next need to figure out your state's requirements for tax-exempt status. This is another area that varies by state. You may also need to do periodic renewals for tax-exempt status.

In Nebraska, you are exempt from income taxes once you receive your IRS Determination Letter.

For sales tax exemption in Nebraska:
Form: 4: Exemption Application for Sales and Use Tax
Submit To: Nebraska Department of Revenue
Cost: $0

Step-12: Charitable Solicitation Registration

This is yet another area where it varies between states, but most require it on an annual basis. This means you need to register with the state before fundraising from any resident of the state. Depending on the scope of your organization you may need to register in other states as well.

This registration is not needed in Nebraska. However, some counties and municipalities may require registration.

Step-13: Business Licenses and Permits

From here you will be all set to start your nonprofit. However, the work isn't over yet. You'll also need to stay in compliance with your nonprofit. Next, consider your required annual filings to remain legal.

Annual Renewal

1. IRS Renewals
    a. IRS Form 990
    b. Due the 15th day of the 5th month following the end of the taxable year.
2. Nebraska has no corporate tax exemption renewal requirements.
3. Nebraska has no sales tax exemption renewal requirements.
4. Nebraska requires a biennial report
    a. Filed with the Nebraska Secretary of State
    b. Filed by mail or online
    c. Costs $20
    d. Due by April 1st of every odd year
    e. Business is dissolved or revoked at 2 months late
    f. Must be filed by a director or officer
    g. Does not need original signatures

NEVADA

Step-1: Name Your Nonprofit

The name of your nonprofit will establish its brand and will allow you to incorporate with the state. The name you choose cannot conflict with any other organization registered within the state of Nevada. Make sure the name you choose is available and meets all state requirement. Search through the Nevada Secretary of State.

Step-2: Choose a Nonprofit Structure

The Nevada Revised Statues offers the following nonprofit structures:
- Nonprofit Corporation
- Nonprofit Cooperative Corporation with Stock
- Nonprofit Cooperative Corporation without Stock
- Corporation Sole
- Cooperative Associations

Step-3: Get Initial Directors and Incorporators

The incorporate is the individual who signs the Articles of Incorporation for your business. You will need at least one incorporator, but you can have additional. The directors are the governing body of your nonprofit and are stakeholders in the purpose and success of your nonprofit. You should have at least three directors who are unrelated individuals in order to meet IRS requirements. You'll also want to meet age and residency requirements.

Step-4: Selected a Registered Agent

The registered agent is responsible for receiving legal notices for your nonprofit. A registered agent needs to be physically living in the state and maintain an office open during regular business hours.

Step-5: Articles of Incorporation

The articles of incorporation are the official creation of your nonprofit. They show where and when the nonprofit was formed and provide the necessary information to verify the nonprofits existence. Make sure your articles of incorporation meet state and IRS requirement.

Form: Articles of Incorporation
Submit To: Nevada Secretary of State
How to File: Mail, fax or in person
Cost: $50. Optional $125-1,000 expedite.
Time Frame: About 1 week. About 24 hours for $125 expedite. About 2 hours for $500 expedite. About 1 hour for $1,000 expedite.

Additional Notes:
- Must be signed by a registered agent
- List of officers/directors needs to be included

Step-6: Get an Employer Identification Number (EIN)

This is a unique nine-digit number that the IRS assigned to identify your nonprofit. Your EIN is then used to open a bank account, apply for 501(c)(3) status and submit 990 IRS returns.

Form: IRS Form SS-4
Submit To: Internal Revenue Service (IRS)

How to File: Mail, phone, fax or online

Cost: $0

Time Frame: By phone or online is immediate, by fax is 4 days and by mail is 4-5 weeks.

Additional Notes:
- Print EIN before the closing session

Step-7: Storing Records

As you start a nonprofit, you will be faced with a number of official documents. Be sure you organize and store all of these records together for easy access later.

Step-8: Initial Governing Policies and Documents

The governing document for your nonprofit is your bylaws since they serve as the operating manual for your organization and need to be consistent with both the law and your articles of incorporation. The first meeting of your Board of Directors should be to review and ratify the bylaws.

You should also create and adopt a conflict of interest policy. This will guide you in what to do if someone in a key position within your nonprofit has competing interests and makes a decision that benefits themselves while harming your nonprofit. Organizational interests should be prioritized ahead of personal interests. All conflicts should be disclosed immediately.

Both the bylaws and the conflict of interest policy will need to be approved and adopted before applying to the IRS for 501(c)(3) status.

Step-9: Board of Directors Organizational Meeting

This initial meeting is the most productive and important one. You will approve bylaws, adopt the conflict of interest policy, elect directors, appoint officers and approve any resolutions like opening a bank account. Be sure to record the decisions made in meeting minutes.

Step-10: State Tax Identification Numbers and Accounts

Incorporating a nonprofit means, you will follow all state laws. Requirements vary by state so check with your individual state first.

To apply in Nevada:

Form: APP-01.00: Nevada Common Business Registration
Submit To: Nevada Department of Taxation
How to File: Mail or online
Cost: $0

Additional Notes:
- Must have your EIN first

Step-11: File for 501(c) Status

This can seem like one of the most difficult steps in starting your nonprofit, but it also offers many benefits. After applying and submitting your documents, the IRS will give you a Determination Letter that officially recognizes your tax-exempt status.

Form: IRS Form 1023, Form 1023-EZ or Form 1024
Submit To: Internal Revenue Service (IRS)
How to File: Mail
Cost: $275 for Form 1023-EZ and $600 for Form 1023

Time Frame: Less than a month for Form 1023-EZ and 3-6 months for Form 1023

Step-12: State Tax Exemption

Once you have your IRS Determination Letter, you next need to figure out your state's requirements for tax-exempt status. This is another area that varies by state. You may also need to do periodic renewals for tax-exempt status.

For state income tax exemption in Nevada:

Form: Exempt Status Entity Form
Submit To: Nevada Department of Taxation
Cost: $0

For sales tax exemption in Nevada:

Form: APP-02.01: Application for Sales/Use Tax Exemption
Submit To: Nevada Department of Taxation
Cost: $0

Step-13: Charitable Solicitation Registration

This is yet another area where it varies between states, but most require it on an annual basis. This means you need to register with the state before fundraising from any resident of the state. Depending on the scope of your organization you may need to register in other states as well.

Overseen By: Nevada Secretary of State

Exemptions:

1. Less than 15 donors annually
2. Solicitation is only within the third degree of personnel of the corporation
3. The corporation is recognized as a church

To file in Nevada, you need to do the following:

Form: Charitable Solicitation Registration Statement (CSRS) or Exemption Form
Submit To: Nevada Secretary of State
How to File: Mail, fax or online
Cost: $0

Additional Notes:
- Attach all personnel names and addresses
- Must be signed by an officer

Step-14: Business Licenses and Permits

From here you will be all set to start your nonprofit. However, the work isn't over yet. You'll also need to stay in compliance with your nonprofit. Next, consider your required annual filings to remain legal.

Annual Renewal

1. IRS Renewals
   a. IRS Form 990
   b. Due the 15th day of the 5th month following the end of the taxable year.
2. Nevada has no corporate tax exemption renewal requirements.
3. Nevada Sales Tax Exemption renewal
   a. Filed with Nevada Department of Taxation
   b. Form APP-02.01: Application for Sales/Use Tax Exemption

    c. Costs $0

    d. Due every 5 years from date of issue

4. Nevada requires an annual list of officers

    a. Filed with the Nevada Secretary of State

    b. Form: Initial/Annual List of Officers and Directors - Nonprofit Corporation

    c. Filed by mail or online

    d. Costs $50

    e. Due by end of registration anniversary month

    f. $50 late fee

    g. May be filed online by anyone with authority. Paper form must be signed by an officer

    h. Does not need original signatures

5. Charitable Solicitation Registration Renewal

    a. Filed with the Nevada Secretary of State

    b. Form Charitable Solicitation Registration Statement (CSRS) or Exemption Form

    c. Filed by mail, fax or online

    d. Costs $0

    e. Due annually at the same time as the annual list of officers

    f. Attach names and addresses of executive personnel

    g. Requires signature of an officer

NEW HAMPSHIRE

Step-1: Name Your Nonprofit

The name of your nonprofit will establish its brand and will allow you to incorporate with the state. The name you choose cannot conflict with any other organization registered within the state of New Hampshire. Make sure the name you choose is available and meets all state requirement. Search through the New Hampshire Secretary of State - Corporations Division.

Step-2: Get Initial Directors and Incorporators

The incorporate is the individual who signs the Articles of Incorporation for your business. You will need at least one incorporator, but you can have additional. The directors are the governing body of your nonprofit and are stakeholders in the purpose and success of your nonprofit. You should have at least three directors who are unrelated individuals in order to meet IRS requirements. You'll also want to meet age and residency requirements.

Step-3: Selected a Registered Agent

The registered agent is responsible for receiving legal notices for your nonprofit. A registered agent needs to be physically living in the state and maintain an office open during regular business hours.

Step-4: Articles of Incorporation

The articles of incorporation are the official creation of your nonprofit. They show where and when the nonprofit was formed and provide the necessary information to verify the

nonprofits existence. Make sure your articles of incorporation meet state and IRS requirement.

Form: NP-1 NH Nonprofit Application
Submit To: New Hampshire Secretary of State - Corporations Division
How to File: Mail
Cost: $25 state fee + $5 city/town fee = $30 total
Time Frame: About 10-14 days

Additional Notes:
- A minimum of five signatures are needed on the Articles of Incorporation
- Submit original copies
- File with the Secretary of State, file a copy with the office of the clerk in the town or city where your corporation is located

Step-5: Get an Employer Identification Number (EIN)

This is a unique nine-digit number that the IRS assigned to identify your nonprofit. Your EIN is then used to open a bank account, apply for 501(c)(3) status and submit 990 IRS returns.

Form: IRS Form SS-4
Submit To: Internal Revenue Service (IRS)
How to File: Mail, phone, fax or online
Cost: $0
Time Frame: By phone or online is immediate, by fax is 4 days and by mail is 4-5 weeks.

Additional Notes:
- Print EIN before the closing session

Step-6: Storing Records

As you start a nonprofit, you will be faced with a number of official documents. Be sure you organize and store all of these records together for easy access later.

Step-7: Initial Governing Policies and Documents

The governing document for your nonprofit is your bylaws since they serve as the operating manual for your organization and need to be consistent with both the law and your articles of incorporation. The first meeting of your Board of Directors should be to review and ratify the bylaws.

You should also create and adopt a conflict of interest policy. This will guide you in what to do if someone in a key position within your nonprofit has competing interests and makes a decision that benefits themselves while harming your nonprofit. Organizational interests should be prioritized ahead of personal interests. All conflicts should be disclosed immediately.

Both the bylaws and the conflict of interest policy will need to be approved and adopted before applying to the IRS for 501(c)(3) status.

Step-8: Board of Directors Organizational Meeting

This initial meeting is the most productive and important one. You will approve bylaws, adopt the conflict of interest policy, elect directors, appoint officers and approve any resolutions like opening a bank account. Be sure to record the decisions made in meeting minutes.

Step-9: State Tax Identification Numbers and Accounts

Incorporating a nonprofit means, you will follow all state laws. Requirements vary by state so check with your individual state first.

To apply in New Hampshire contact the New Hampshire Department of Revenue Administration.

Step-10: File for 501(c) Status

This can seem like one of the most difficult steps in starting your nonprofit, but it also offers many benefits. After applying and submitting your documents, the IRS will give you a Determination Letter that officially recognizes your tax-exempt status.

Form: IRS Form 1023, Form 1023-EZ or Form 1024
Submit To: Internal Revenue Service (IRS)
How to File: Mail
Cost: $275 for Form 1023-EZ and $600 for Form 1023
Time Frame: Less than a month for Form 1023-EZ and 3-6 months for Form 1023

Step-11: State Tax Exemption

Once you have your IRS Determination Letter, you next need to figure out your state's requirements for tax-exempt status. This is another area that varies by state. You may also need to do periodic renewals for tax-exempt status.

There is no need to apply for state income tax exemption in New Hampshire.

There is no state-level sales tax in New Hampshire.

Step-12: Charitable Solicitation Registration
This is yet another area where it varies between states, but most require it on an annual basis. This means you need to register with the state before fundraising from any resident of the state. Depending on the scope of your organization you may need to register in other states as well.

Overseen By: New Hampshire Department of Justice - Charitable Trusts Unit

Exemptions:
1. Religious organizations

To file in New Hampshire, you need to do the following:

Form: URS or NHCT-1: Application for Registration
Submit To: New Hampshire Department of Justice - Charitable Trusts Unit
How to File: Mail
Cost: $25

Additional Notes:
- Attach all necessary documents
- If filing the URS, attach a conflict of interest policy
- Must be signed by the president and treasurer
- Signatures don't need to be notarized
- You will receive a Certificate of Registration when approved

Step-13: Business Licenses and Permits

From here you will be all set to start your nonprofit. However, the work isn't over yet. You'll also need to stay in compliance with your nonprofit. Next, consider your required annual filings to remain legal.

Annual Renewal

1. IRS Renewals
    a. IRS Form 990
    b. Due the 15th day of the 5th month following the end of the taxable year.

2. New Hampshire Corporate Tax Returns
    a. Filed with New Hampshire Department of Revenue Administration
    b. Form BET (Business Enterprise Tax)
    c. Due two and a half months after fiscal year end
3. New Hampshire has no corporate tax exemption renewal requirements.
4. New Hampshire has no state-level sales tax.
5. New Hampshire requires the filing of a return
    a. Filed with the New Hampshire Secretary of State - Corporations Division
    b. The form is mailed to you
    c. Filed by mail or online
    d. Costs $25
    e. Due by December 31st every 5 years
6. Charitable Solicitation Registration Renewal
    a. Filed with the New Hampshire Department of Justice - Charitable Trusts Unit
    b. IRS Form 990 or Form NHCT-2A: Annual Report
    c. Filed by mail
    d. Costs $75
    e. Due annually four and a half months after the close of the fiscal year
    f. Attach necessary documents; larger corporations need to provide financial statements
    g. Must be signed by the president and treasurer
    h. Doesn't need to be notarized
    i. Confirmation not provided by the state

NEW JERSEY

Step-1: Name Your Nonprofit

The name of your nonprofit will establish its brand and will allow you to incorporate with the state. The name you choose cannot conflict with any other organization registered within the state of New Jersey. Make sure the name you choose is available and meets all state requirement. Search through the New Jersey Department of Treasury.

Step-2: Get Initial Directors and Incorporators

The incorporate is the individual who signs the Articles of Incorporation for your business. You will need at least one incorporator, but you can have additional. The directors are the governing body of your nonprofit and are stakeholders in the purpose and success of your nonprofit. You should have at least three directors who are unrelated individuals in order to meet IRS requirements. You'll also want to meet age and residency requirements.

Step-3: Selected a Registered Agent

The registered agent is responsible for receiving legal notices for your nonprofit. A registered agent needs to be physically living in the state and maintain an office open during regular business hours.

Step-4: Articles of Incorporation

The articles of incorporation are the official creation of your nonprofit. They show where and when the nonprofit was formed and provide the necessary information to verify the nonprofits existence. Make sure your articles of incorporation meet state and IRS requirement.

Form: Public Records Filing for New Business Entity
Submit To: New Jersey Department of Treasury
How to File: Mail, in person, fax or online
Cost: $75
Time Frame: About 4 weeks. Expedited available.

Additional Notes:
- Include a cover letter or self-addressed stamped envelope for return

Step-5: Get an Employer Identification Number (EIN)

This is a unique nine-digit number that the IRS assigned to identify your nonprofit. Your EIN is then used to open a bank account, apply for 501(c)(3) status and submit 990 IRS returns.

Form: IRS Form SS-4
Submit To: Internal Revenue Service (IRS)
How to File: Mail, phone, fax or online
Cost: $0
Time Frame: By phone or online is immediate, by fax is 4 days and by mail is 4-5 weeks.

Additional Notes:
- Print EIN before the closing session

Step-6: Storing Records

As you start a nonprofit, you will be faced with a number of official documents. Be sure you organize and store all of these records together for easy access later.

Step-7: Initial Governing Policies and Documents

The governing document for your nonprofit is your bylaws since they serve as the operating manual for your organization and need to be consistent with both the law and your articles of incorporation. The first meeting of your Board of Directors should be to review and ratify the bylaws.

You should also create and adopt a conflict of interest policy. This will guide you in what to do if someone in a key position within your nonprofit has competing interests and makes a decision that benefits themselves while harming your nonprofit. Organizational interests should be prioritized ahead of personal interests. All conflicts should be disclosed immediately.

Both the bylaws and the conflict of interest policy will need to be approved and adopted before applying to the IRS for 501(c)(3) status.

Step-8: Board of Directors Organizational Meeting

This initial meeting is the most productive and important one. You will approve bylaws, adopt the conflict of interest policy, elect directors, appoint officers and approve any resolutions like opening a bank account. Be sure to record the decisions made in meeting minutes.

Step-9: State Tax Identification Numbers and Accounts

Incorporating a nonprofit means, you will follow all state laws. Requirements vary by state so check with your individual state first.
To apply in New Jersey:

Form: NJ-REG: Business Registration Form
Submit To: State of New Jersey - Department of the Treasury
How to File: Mail or online

Cost: $0

Additional Notes:
- Submit within 60 days of filing business entity

Step-10: File for 501(c) Status

This can seem like one of the most difficult steps in starting your nonprofit, but it also offers many benefits. After applying and submitting your documents, the IRS will give you a Determination Letter that officially recognizes your tax-exempt status.

Form: IRS Form 1023, Form 1023-EZ or Form 1024
Submit To: Internal Revenue Service (IRS)
How to File: Mail
Cost: $275 for Form 1023-EZ and $600 for Form 1023
Time Frame: Less than a month for Form 1023-EZ and 3-6 months for Form 1023

Step-11: State Tax Exemption

Once you have your IRS Determination Letter, you next need to figure out your state's requirements for tax-exempt status. This is another area that varies by state. You may also need to do periodic renewals for tax-exempt status.

There is no need to apply for state income tax exemption in New Jersey.
To apply for state sales tax exemption in New Jersey:

Form: REG-1E: Application for Exempt Organization Certificate
Submit To: New Jersey Department of the Treasury - Division of Taxation
Costs: $0

Step-12: Charitable Solicitation Registration

This is yet another area where it varies between states, but most require it on an annual basis. This means you need to register with the state before fundraising from any resident of the state. Depending on the scope of your organization you may need to register in other states as well.

Overseen By: New Jersey Division of Consumer Affairs - Charities Registration Section

Exemptions:
1. Less than $10,000 gross contributions per fiscal year
2. Religious organizations
3. Educational institutions
4. The local unit of a parent organization

To file in New Jersey, you need to do the following:

Form: URS or Form CRI-200: Short Form Registration / Verification Statement or Form CRI-150I: Long Form Initial Registration Statement
Submit To: New Hampshire Department of Justice - Charitable Trusts Unit
How to File: Mail
Cost: $30-250 depending on gross contributions

Additional Notes:
- Attach all necessary documents
- Must be signed by the CFO and another authorized officer
- Signatures don't need to be notarized

Step-13: Business Licenses and Permits

From here you will be all set to start your nonprofit. However, the work isn't over yet. You'll also need to stay in compliance with your nonprofit. Next, consider your required annual filings to remain legal.

Annual Renewal

1. IRS Renewals
    a. IRS Form 990
    b. Due the 15th day of the 5th month following the end of the taxable year.
2. New Jersey has no corporate tax exemption renewal requirements.
3. New Jersey has no state-level sales tax.
4. New Jersey requires the filing of an annual report
    a. Filed with the New Jersey Department of Treasury
    b. Filed online
    c. Costs $27
    d. Due annually by date of incorporation/registration
    e. Any authorized individual can file
5. Charitable Solicitation Registration Renewal
    a. Filed with the New Jersey Division of Consumer Affairs - Charities Registration Section
    b. URS or Form CRI-200: Short Form Registration / Verification Statement or Form CRI-150I: Long Form Initial Registration Statement
    c. Filed by mail
    d. Costs $30-250 depending on gross contributions
    e. Due annually six months after the end of the fiscal year
    f. Attach necessary documents; larger corporations need to provide financial statements

NEW MEXICO

Step-1: Name Your Nonprofit

The name of your nonprofit will establish its brand and will allow you to incorporate with the state. The name you choose cannot conflict with any other organization registered within the state of New Mexico. Make sure the name you choose is available and meets all state requirement. Search through the New Mexico Secretary of State - Corporations Bureau.

Step-2: Get Initial Directors and Incorporators

The incorporate is the individual who signs the Articles of Incorporation for your business. You will need at least one incorporator, but you can have additional. The directors are the governing body of your nonprofit and are stakeholders in the purpose and success of your nonprofit. You should have at least three directors who are unrelated individuals in order to meet IRS requirements. You'll also want to meet age and residency requirements.

Step-3: Selected a Registered Agent

The registered agent is responsible for receiving legal notices for your nonprofit. A registered agent needs to be physically living in the state and maintain an office open during regular business hours.

Step-4: Articles of Incorporation

The articles of incorporation are the official creation of your nonprofit. They show where and when the nonprofit was formed and provide the necessary information to verify the

nonprofits existence. Make sure your articles of incorporation meet state and IRS requirement.

Form: Articles of Incorporation
Submit To: New Mexico Secretary of State - Corporations Bureau
How to File: Mail, in person or fax
Cost: $25. Optional $100-150 expedite.
Time Frame: About 3 months. About 2 days for $100 expedite. About 1 day for $150 expedite.

Additional Notes:
- File a signed original, one copy, one registered agent statement and the filing fee
- Must file within 30 days of being issued your Certificate of Incorporation

Step-5: Get an Employer Identification Number (EIN)

This is a unique nine-digit number that the IRS assigned to identify your nonprofit. Your EIN is then used to open a bank account, apply for 501(c)(3) status and submit 990 IRS returns.

Form: IRS Form SS-4
Submit To: Internal Revenue Service (IRS)
How to File: Mail, phone, fax or online
Cost: $0
Time Frame: By phone or online is immediate, by fax is 4 days and by mail is 4-5 weeks.

Additional Notes:
- Print EIN before the closing session

Step-6: Storing Records

As you start a nonprofit, you will be faced with a number of official documents. Be sure you organize and store all of these records together for easy access later.

Step-7: Initial Governing Policies and Documents

The governing document for your nonprofit is your bylaws since they serve as the operating manual for your organization and need to be consistent with both the law and your articles of incorporation. The first meeting of your Board of Directors should be to review and ratify the bylaws.

You should also create and adopt a conflict of interest policy. This will guide you in what to do if someone in a key position within your nonprofit has competing interests and makes a decision that benefits themselves while harming your nonprofit. Organizational interests should be prioritized ahead of personal interests. All conflicts should be disclosed immediately.

Both the bylaws and the conflict of interest policy will need to be approved and adopted before applying to the IRS for 501(c)(3) status.

Step-8: Board of Directors Organizational Meeting

This initial meeting is the most productive and important one. You will approve bylaws, adopt the conflict of interest policy, elect directors, appoint officers and approve any resolutions like opening a bank account. Be sure to record the decisions made in meeting minutes.

Step-9: State Tax Identification Numbers and Accounts

Incorporating a nonprofit means, you will follow all state laws. Requirements vary by state so check with your individual state first.

To apply in New Mexico:

Form: ACD-31015: Application for Business Tax Identification Number
Submit To: New Mexico Taxation and Revenue Department
How to File: Mail or online
Cost: $0

Step-10: File for 501(c) Status

This can seem like one of the most difficult steps in starting your nonprofit, but it also offers many benefits. After applying and submitting your documents, the IRS will give you a Determination Letter that officially recognizes your tax-exempt status.

Form: IRS Form 1023, Form 1023-EZ or Form 1024
Submit To: Internal Revenue Service (IRS)
How to File: Mail
Cost: $275 for Form 1023-EZ and $600 for Form 1023
Time Frame: Less than a month for Form 1023-EZ and 3-6 months for Form 1023

Step-11: State Tax Exemption

Once you have your IRS Determination Letter, you next need to figure out your state's requirements for tax-exempt status. This is another area that varies by state. You may also need to do periodic renewals for tax-exempt status.

There is no need to apply for state income tax exemption in New Mexico.
There is no need to apply for state sales tax exemption in New Mexico.

Step-12: Charitable Solicitation Registration

This is yet another area where it varies between states, but most require it on an annual basis. This means you need to register with the state before fundraising from any resident of the state. Depending on the scope of your organization you may need to register in other states as well.

Overseen By: New Mexico Attorney General - Charities Unit

Exemptions:
1. Appeals for named individuals
2. Religious organizations
3. Educational institutions

To file in New Mexico, you need to do the following:

Form: NM-COROS
Submit To: New Mexico Attorney General - Charities Unit
How to File: Online
Cost: $0

Additional Notes:
- Due within 30 days of incorporation
- Signed by the CFO

Step-13: Business Licenses and Permits

From here you will be all set to start your nonprofit. However, the work isn't over yet. You'll also need to stay in compliance with your nonprofit. Next, consider your required annual filings to remain legal.

Annual Renewal

1. IRS Renewals
    a. IRS Form 990
    b. Due the 15th day of the 5th month following the end of the taxable year.
2. New Mexico has no corporate tax exemption renewal requirements.
3. New Mexico has no state-level sales tax.
4. New Mexico requires the filing of an annual report
    a. Filed with the New Mexico Secretary of State - Corporations Bureau
    b. Filed online
    c. Costs $10
    d. Due annually by 4 months and 15 days after the close of the taxable year
    e. $10 late fee
    f. May be filed by any officer
5. Charitable Solicitation Registration Renewal
    a. Filed with the New Mexico Attorney General - Charities Unit
    b. Filed by online
    c. Costs $0
    d. Due annually six months after the end of the fiscal year

NEW YORK

Step-1: Name Your Nonprofit

The name of your nonprofit will establish its brand and will allow you to incorporate with the state. The name you choose cannot conflict with any other organization registered within the state of New York. Make sure the name you choose is available and meets all state requirement. Search through the New York Department of State - Division of Corporations, State Records, and Uniform Commercial Code.

Step-2: Choose a Nonprofit Corporation Structure

There are two types of nonprofit structures in New York: Religious and Non-Religious Corporations.

Step-3: Get Initial Directors and Incorporators

The incorporate is the individual who signs the Articles of Incorporation for your business. You will need at least one incorporator, but you can have additional. The directors are the governing body of your nonprofit and are stakeholders in the purpose and success of your nonprofit. You should have at least three directors who are unrelated individuals in order to meet IRS requirements. You'll also want to meet age and residency requirements.

Step-4: Selected a Registered Agent

The registered agent is responsible for receiving legal notices for your nonprofit. A registered agent needs to be physically living in the state and maintain an office open during regular business hours.

Step-5: Obtains NY Agency Approval

Based on the table below see which agency you need to get written consent from.

Nonprofit Purpose	NY Agency
Trade or business association	Office of the Attorney General - Antitrust Bureau
Program for children or elderly	Office of Children and Family Services
Adult care facility	Department of Health - Division of Legal Affairs
General education purposes	NYS Department of Education - Office of Counsel
Health facilities	Department of Health - Division of Legal Affairs
Mental health	Office of Mental Health - Bureau of Inspection and Certification
Mental rehabilitation	Office for People with Developmental Disabilities - Office of Counsel
Alcohol or substance abuse	Office of Alcoholism and Substance Abuse Services

Step-6: Articles of Incorporation

The articles of incorporation are the official creation of your nonprofit. They show where and when the nonprofit was formed and provide the necessary information to verify the nonprofits existence. Make sure your articles of incorporation meet state and IRS requirement.

Form: Certificate of Incorporation

Submit To: New York Department of State - Division of Corporations, State Records, and Uniform Commercial Code

How to File: Mail, in person or fax

Cost: $75. Optional $25-150 expedite.

Time Frame: About 14 days. Within 24 hours for $25 expedite. Same day for $75 expedite. Within 2 hours for $150 expedite.

Step-7: Get an Employer Identification Number (EIN)

This is a unique nine-digit number that the IRS assigned to identify your nonprofit. Your EIN is then used to open a bank account, apply for 501(c)(3) status and submit 990 IRS returns.

Form: IRS Form SS-4

Submit To: Internal Revenue Service (IRS)

How to File: Mail, phone, fax or online

Cost: $0

Time Frame: By phone or online is immediate, by fax is 4 days and by mail is 4-5 weeks.

Additional Notes:
- Print EIN before the closing session

Step-8: Storing Records

As you start a nonprofit, you will be faced with a number of official documents. Be sure you organize and store all of these records together for easy access later.

Step-9: Initial Governing Policies and Documents

The governing document for your nonprofit is your bylaws since they serve as the operating manual for your organization and need to be consistent with both the law and your articles of incorporation. The first meeting of your Board of Directors should be to review and ratify the bylaws.

You should also create and adopt a conflict of interest policy. This will guide you in what to do if someone in a key position within your nonprofit has competing interests and makes a decision that benefits themselves while harming your nonprofit. Organizational interests should be prioritized ahead of personal interests. All conflicts should be disclosed immediately.

Both the bylaws and the conflict of interest policy will need to be approved and adopted before applying to the IRS for 501(c)(3) status.

Step-10: Board of Directors Organizational Meeting

This initial meeting is the most productive and important one. You will approve bylaws, adopt the conflict of interest policy, elect directors, appoint officers and approve any resolutions like opening a bank account. Be sure to record the decisions made in meeting minutes.

Step-11: State Tax Identification Numbers and Accounts

Incorporating a nonprofit means, you will follow all state laws. Requirements vary by state so check with your individual state first.
To apply in New York contact the NYS Department of Taxation and Finance

Step-12: File for 501(c) Status

This can seem like one of the most difficult steps in starting your nonprofit, but it also offers many benefits. After applying and submitting your documents, the IRS will give you a Determination Letter that officially recognizes your tax-exempt status.

Form: IRS Form 1023, Form 1023-EZ or Form 1024
Submit To: Internal Revenue Service (IRS)
How to File: Mail
Cost: $275 for Form 1023-EZ and $600 for Form 1023
Time Frame: Less than a month for Form 1023-EZ and 3-6 months for Form 1023

Step-13: State Tax Exemption

Once you have your IRS Determination Letter, you next need to figure out your state's requirements for tax-exempt status. This is another area that varies by state. You may also need to do periodic renewals for tax-exempt status.

To file for state income tax exemption in New York:

Form: CT-247: Application for Exemption from Corporation Franchise Taxes by a Not-for-Profit Organization
Submit To: New York State Department of Taxation and Finance
Cost: $0

To file for state sales tax exemption in New York:

Form: ST-119.2: Application for an Exempt Organization Certificate
Submit To: New York State Department of Taxation and Finances
Cost: $0

Step-14: Charitable Solicitation Registration

This is yet another area where it varies between states, but most require it on an annual basis. This means you need to register with the state before fundraising from any resident of the state. Depending on the scope of your organization you may need to register in other states as well.

Overseen By: New York Attorney General - Charities Bureau

Exemptions:
1. Appeals for named individuals
2. Religious organizations
3. Educational institutions
4. Less than $25,000 contributions per year
5. PTAs
6. Membership organizations

To file in New York, you need to do the following:

Form: CHAR410: Registration Statement for Charitable Organizations
Submit To: New York Attorney General - Charities Bureau
How to File: Mail
Cost: $25

Additional Notes:
- Attached necessary documents
- Must be signed by the president and CFO/treasurer
- Doesn't need to be notarized

Step-15: Business Licenses and Permits

From here you will be all set to start your nonprofit. However, the work isn't over yet. You'll also need to stay in compliance with your nonprofit. Next, consider your required annual filings to remain legal.

Annual Renewal

1. IRS Renewals
    a. IRS Form 990
    b. Due the 15th day of the 5th month following the end of the taxable year.
2. New York has no corporate tax exemption renewal requirements.
3. New York has no state-level sales tax.
4. New York doesn't require the filing of an annual report
5. Charitable Solicitation Registration Renewal
    a. Filed with the New York Attorney General - Charities Bureau
    b. Form CHAR500: Annual Filing for Charitable Organizations
    c. Filed by mail or online
    d. Costs $10-25 based on total support and revenue
    e. Due annually four and a half months after the end of the fiscal year
    f. Attach all necessary documents

NORTH CAROLINA

Step-1: Name Your Nonprofit

The name of your nonprofit will establish its brand and will allow you to incorporate with the state. The name you choose cannot conflict with any other organization registered within the state of North Carolina. Make sure the name you choose is available and meets all state requirement. Search through the North Carolina Secretary of State - Business Registration Division.

Step-2: Get Initial Directors and Incorporators

The incorporate is the individual who signs the Articles of Incorporation for your business. You will need at least one incorporator, but you can have additional. The directors are the governing body of your nonprofit and are stakeholders in the purpose and success of your nonprofit. You should have at least three directors who are unrelated individuals in order to meet IRS requirements. You'll also want to meet age and residency requirements.

Step-3: Selected a Registered Agent

The registered agent is responsible for receiving legal notices for your nonprofit. A registered agent needs to be physically living in the state and maintain an office open during regular business hours.

Step-4: Articles of Incorporation

The articles of incorporation are the official creation of your nonprofit. They show where and when the nonprofit was formed and provide the necessary information to verify the

nonprofits existence. Make sure your articles of incorporation meet state and IRS requirement.

Form: N-01: Articles of Incorporation for Nonprofit
Submit To: North Carolina Secretary of State - Business Registration Division
How to File: Mail, in person or online
Cost: $60. Optional $100-200 expedite.
Time Frame: About 5-7 days. 24 hours with $100 expedite. Same day with $200 expedite.

Step-5: Get an Employer Identification Number (EIN)

This is a unique nine-digit number that the IRS assigned to identify your nonprofit. Your EIN is then used to open a bank account, apply for 501(c)(3) status and submit 990 IRS returns.

Form: IRS Form SS-4
Submit To: Internal Revenue Service (IRS)
How to File: Mail, phone, fax or online
Cost: $0
Time Frame: By phone or online is immediate, by fax is 4 days and by mail is 4-5 weeks.

Additional Notes:
- Print EIN before the closing session

Step-6: Storing Records

As you start a nonprofit, you will be faced with a number of official documents. Be sure you organize and store all of these records together for easy access later.

Step-7: Initial Governing Policies and Documents

The governing document for your nonprofit is your bylaws since they serve as the operating manual for your organization and need to be consistent with both the law and your articles of incorporation. The first meeting of your Board of Directors should be to review and ratify the bylaws.

You should also create and adopt a conflict of interest policy. This will guide you in what to do if someone in a key position within your nonprofit has competing interests and makes a decision that benefits themselves while harming your nonprofit. Organizational interests should be prioritized ahead of personal interests. All conflicts should be disclosed immediately.

Both the bylaws and the conflict of interest policy will need to be approved and adopted before applying to the IRS for 501(c)(3) status.

Step-8: Board of Directors Organizational Meeting

This initial meeting is the most productive and important one. You will approve bylaws, adopt the conflict of interest policy, elect directors, appoint officers and approve any resolutions like opening a bank account. Be sure to record the decisions made in meeting minutes.

Step-9: State Tax Identification Numbers and Accounts

Incorporating a nonprofit means, you will follow all state laws. Requirements vary by state so check with your individual state first.

To file in North Carolina:

Form: NC-BR: Business Registration Application for Income Tax Withholding, Sales and Use Tax, and Machinery and Equipment Tax

Submit To: North Carolina Department of Revenue
How to File: Mail or online
Cost: $0

Step-10: File for 501(c) Status

This can seem like one of the most difficult steps in starting your nonprofit, but it also offers many benefits. After applying and submitting your documents, the IRS will give you a Determination Letter that officially recognizes your tax-exempt status.

Form: IRS Form 1023, Form 1023-EZ or Form 1024
Submit To: Internal Revenue Service (IRS)
How to File: Mail
Cost: $275 for Form 1023-EZ and $600 for Form 1023
Time Frame: Less than a month for Form 1023-EZ and 3-6 months for Form 1023

Step-11: State Tax Exemption

Once you have your IRS Determination Letter, you next need to figure out your state's requirements for tax-exempt status. This is another area that varies by state. You may also need to do periodic renewals for tax-exempt status.

To file for state income tax exemption in North Carolina contact the North Carolina Department of Revenue.

North Carolina does not offer a sales tax exemption for nonprofits.

Step-12: Charitable Solicitation Registration

This is yet another area where it varies between states, but most require it on an annual basis. This means you need to register with the state before fundraising from any resident of the state. Depending on the scope of your organization you may need to register in other states as well.

Overseen By: North Carolina Secretary of State - Charitable Solicitation Licensing Division

Exemptions:
1. Less than $25,000 contributions per year
2. Religious organizations
3. Educational institutions

To file in North Carolina, you need to do the following:

Form: Initial / Renewal License Application for Charities or Sponsors
Submit To: North Carolina Secretary of State - Charitable Solicitation Licensing Division
How to File: Mail
Cost: $0-200 depending on contributions

Additional Notes:
- Attach all necessary documents
- Must be signed by the CFO/treasurer
- Must be notarized

Step-13: Business Licenses and Permits

From here you will be all set to start your nonprofit. However, the work isn't over yet. You'll also need to stay in compliance with your nonprofit. Next, consider your required annual filings to remain legal.

Annual Renewal

1. IRS Renewals
   a. IRS Form 990
   b. Due the 15th day of the 5th month following the end of the taxable year.
2. North Carolina has no renewal requirements for corporate income tax exemption.
3. North Carolina Sales Tax Returns
   a. Filed with North Carolina Department of Revenue
   b. Form E-585 (Sales Tax Refund)
   c. Cost $0
   d. Due April 15th and October 15th
4. North Carolina has no renewal requirements for sales tax exemption.
5. North Carolina doesn't require an annual report.
6. Charitable Solicitation Renewal
   a. Filed with the North Carolina Secretary of State - Charitable Solicitation Licensing Division
   b. Form Initial / Renewal License Application for Charities or Sponsors
   c. Filed by mail
   d. Costs $0-200 depending on contributions
   e. Due annually four and a half months after the close of the fiscal year
   f. Attach all necessary documents

NORTH DAKOTA

Step-1: Name Your Nonprofit

The name of your nonprofit will establish its brand and will allow you to incorporate with the state. The name you choose cannot conflict with any other organization registered within the state of North Dakota. Make sure the name you choose is available and meets all state requirement. Search through the North Dakota Secretary of State.

Step-2: Get Initial Directors and Incorporators

The incorporate is the individual who signs the Articles of Incorporation for your business. You will need at least one incorporator, but you can have additional. The directors are the governing body of your nonprofit and are stakeholders in the purpose and success of your nonprofit. You should have at least three directors who are unrelated individuals in order to meet IRS requirements. You'll also want to meet age and residency requirements.

Step-3: Selected a Registered Agent

The registered agent is responsible for receiving legal notices for your nonprofit. A registered agent needs to be physically living in the state and maintain an office open during regular business hours.

Step-4: Articles of Incorporation

The articles of incorporation are the official creation of your nonprofit. They show where and when the nonprofit was formed and provide the necessary information to verify the nonprofits existence. Make sure your articles of incorporation meet state and IRS requirement.

Form: North Dakota Nonprofit Corporation Articles of Incorporation (SFN 13003)
Submit To: North Dakota Secretary of State
How to File: Mail or fax
Cost: $40
Time Frame: About 30 days. No, expedite available.

Step-5: Get an Employer Identification Number (EIN)

This is a unique nine-digit number that the IRS assigned to identify your nonprofit. Your EIN is then used to open a bank account, apply for 501(c)(3) status and submit 990 IRS returns.

Form: IRS Form SS-4
Submit To: Internal Revenue Service (IRS)
How to File: Mail, phone, fax or online
Cost: $0
Time Frame: By phone or online is immediate, by fax is 4 days and by mail is 4-5 weeks.

Additional Notes:
- Print EIN before the closing session

Step-6: Storing Records

As you start a nonprofit, you will be faced with a number of official documents. Be sure you organize and store all of these records together for easy access later.

Step-7: Initial Governing Policies and Documents

The governing document for your nonprofit is your bylaws since they serve as the operating manual for your organization and need to be consistent with both the law and

your articles of incorporation. The first meeting of your Board of Directors should be to review and ratify the bylaws.

You should also create and adopt a conflict of interest policy. This will guide you in what to do if someone in a key position within your nonprofit has competing interests and makes a decision that benefits themselves while harming your nonprofit. Organizational interests should be prioritized ahead of personal interests. All conflicts should be disclosed immediately.

Both the bylaws and the conflict of interest policy will need to be approved and adopted before applying to the IRS for 501(c)(3) status.

Step-8: Board of Directors Organizational Meeting

This initial meeting is the most productive and important one. You will approve bylaws, adopt the conflict of interest policy, elect directors, appoint officers and approve any resolutions like opening a bank account. Be sure to record the decisions made in meeting minutes.

Step-9: State Tax Identification Numbers and Accounts

Incorporating a nonprofit means, you will follow all state laws. Requirements vary by state so check with your individual state first.

To file in North Dakota:

Submit To: North Dakota Office of State Tax Commissioner
How to File: Mail
Cost: $0

Step-10: File for 501(c) Status

This can seem like one of the most difficult steps in starting your nonprofit, but it also offers many benefits. After applying and submitting your documents, the IRS will give you a Determination Letter that officially recognizes your tax-exempt status.

Form: IRS Form 1023, Form 1023-EZ or Form 1024
Submit To: Internal Revenue Service (IRS)
How to File: Mail
Cost: $275 for Form 1023-EZ and $600 for Form 1023
Time Frame: Less than a month for Form 1023-EZ and 3-6 months for Form 1023

Step-11: State Tax Exemption

Once you have your IRS Determination Letter, you next need to figure out your state's requirements for tax-exempt status. This is another area that varies by state. You may also need to do periodic renewals for tax-exempt status.

North Dakota doesn't require filing for income tax exemption.

North Dakota doesn't require filing for sales tax exemption.

Step-12: Charitable Solicitation Registration

This is yet another area where it varies between states, but most require it on an annual basis. This means you need to register with the state before fundraising from any resident of the state. Depending on the scope of your organization you may need to register in other states as well.

Overseen By: North Dakota Secretary of State

Exemptions:
1. Appeals for named organizations
2. Religious organizations
3. Educational institutions
4. Political organizations

To file in Dakota, you need to do the following:

Form: URS and/or Form SFN 11300: Charitable Organization Registration Statement
Submit To: North Dakota Secretary of State
How to File: Mail
Cost: $25

Additional Notes:
- Attach all necessary documents
- Must be signed by one officer
- Must be notarized

Step-13: Business Licenses and Permits

From here you will be all set to start your nonprofit. However, the work isn't over yet. You'll also need to stay in compliance with your nonprofit. Next, consider your required annual filings to remain legal.

Annual Renewal

1. IRS Renewals
    a. IRS Form 990
    b. Due the 15th day of the 5th month following the end of the taxable year.
2. North Dakota has no renewal requirements for corporate income tax exemption.

3. North Dakota has no renewal requirements for sales tax exemption.
4. North Dakota requires the filing of an annual report
    a. Filed with North Dakota Secretary of State
    b. Filed by mail or fax
    c. Costs $10
    d. Due annually by February 1st
    e. $5 late fee
    f. May be filed by anyone with authority
    g. Doesn't need original signatures
5. Charitable Solicitation Renewal
    a. Filed with the North Dakota Secretary of State
    b. Form SFN 11302: Charitable Organization Annual Report
    c. Filed by mail
    d. Costs $10
    e. Due annually by September 1st
    f. Attach all necessary documents

OHIO

Step-1: Name Your Nonprofit

The name of your nonprofit will establish its brand and will allow you to incorporate with the state. The name you choose cannot conflict with any other organization registered within the state of Ohio. Make sure the name you choose is available and meets all state requirement. Search through the Ohio Secretary of State.

Step-2: Get Initial Directors and Incorporators

The incorporate is the individual who signs the Articles of Incorporation for your business. You will need at least one incorporator, but you can have additional. The directors are the governing body of your nonprofit and are stakeholders in the purpose and success of your nonprofit. You should have at least three directors who are unrelated individuals in order to meet IRS requirements. You'll also want to meet age and residency requirements.

Step-3: Selected a Registered Agent

The registered agent is responsible for receiving legal notices for your nonprofit. A registered agent needs to be physically living in the state and maintain an office open during regular business hours.

Step-4: Articles of Incorporation

The articles of incorporation are the official creation of your nonprofit. They show where and when the nonprofit was formed and provide the necessary information to verify the nonprofits existence. Make sure your articles of incorporation meet state and IRS requirement.

Form: 532B: Initial Articles of Incorporation

Submit To: Ohio Secretary of State

How to File: Mail or online

Cost: $99

Time Frame: About 3-7 days by mail

Additional Notes:
- Must be signed by the registered agent

Step-5: Get an Employer Identification Number (EIN)

This is a unique nine-digit number that the IRS assigned to identify your nonprofit. Your EIN is then used to open a bank account, apply for 501(c)(3) status and submit 990 IRS returns.

Form: IRS Form SS-4

Submit To: Internal Revenue Service (IRS)

How to File: Mail, phone, fax or online

Cost: $0

Time Frame: By phone or online is immediate, by fax is 4 days and by mail is 4-5 weeks.

Additional Notes:
- Print EIN before the closing session

Step-6: Storing Records

As you start a nonprofit, you will be faced with a number of official documents. Be sure you organize and store all of these records together for easy access later.

Step-7: Initial Governing Policies and Documents

The governing document for your nonprofit is your bylaws since they serve as the operating manual for your organization and need to be consistent with both the law and your articles of incorporation. The first meeting of your Board of Directors should be to review and ratify the bylaws.

You should also create and adopt a conflict of interest policy. This will guide you in what to do if someone in a key position within your nonprofit has competing interests and makes a decision that benefits themselves while harming your nonprofit. Organizational interests should be prioritized ahead of personal interests. All conflicts should be disclosed immediately.

Both the bylaws and the conflict of interest policy will need to be approved and adopted before applying to the IRS for 501(c)(3) status.

Step-8: Board of Directors Organizational Meeting

This initial meeting is the most productive and important one. You will approve bylaws, adopt the conflict of interest policy, elect directors, appoint officers and approve any resolutions like opening a bank account. Be sure to record the decisions made in meeting minutes.

Step-9: State Tax Identification Numbers and Accounts

Incorporating a nonprofit means, you will follow all state laws. Requirements vary by state so check with your individual state first.

To file in Ohio contact the Ohio Department of Taxation.

Step-10: File for 501(c) Status

This can seem like one of the most difficult steps in starting your nonprofit, but it also offers many benefits. After applying and submitting your documents, the IRS will give you a Determination Letter that officially recognizes your tax-exempt status.

Form: IRS Form 1023, Form 1023-EZ or Form 1024
Submit To: Internal Revenue Service (IRS)
How to File: Mail
Cost: $275 for Form 1023-EZ and $600 for Form 1023
Time Frame: Less than a month for Form 1023-EZ and 3-6 months for Form 1023

Step-11: State Tax Exemption

Once you have your IRS Determination Letter, you next need to figure out your state's requirements for tax-exempt status. This is another area that varies by state. You may also need to do periodic renewals for tax-exempt status.

Ohio doesn't require filing for income tax exemption.

Ohio doesn't require filing for sales tax exemption.

Step-12: Charitable Solicitation Registration

This is yet another area where it varies between states, but most require it on an annual basis. This means you need to register with the state before fundraising from any resident of the state. Depending on the scope of your organization you may need to register in other states as well.

Overseen By: Ohio Attorney General
Exemptions:
1. Less than $25,000 nationwide gross revenue in the previous fiscal year
2. Religious organizations

3. Educational institutions
4. Membership organizations

To file in Ohio, you need to do the following:

Submit To: Ohio Attorney General
How to File: Online
Cost: $0-200 depending on contributions

Additional Notes:
- Attach all necessary documents
- Must be signed by CFO/treasurer

Step-13: Business Licenses and Permits

From here you will be all set to start your nonprofit. However, the work isn't over yet. You'll also need to stay in compliance with your nonprofit. Next, consider your required annual filings to remain legal.

Annual Renewal

1. IRS Renewals
    a. IRS Form 990
    b. Due the 15th day of the 5th month following the end of the taxable year.
2. Ohio has no renewal requirements for corporate income tax exemption.
3. Ohio has no renewal requirements for sales tax exemption.
4. Ohio requires a statement of continued existence
    a. Filed with Ohio Secretary of State
    b. Form Statement of Continued Existence
    c. Filed by mail or online

d. Costs $25
   e. Due every five years by the end of the registration anniversary month
   f. Must be filed by two officers or three members
   g. Doesn't need original signatures
5. Charitable Solicitation Renewal
   a. Filed with the Ohio Attorney General
   b. Filed online
   c. Costs $0-200 depending on contributions
   d. Due annually four and a half months after the end of the fiscal year
   e. $200 late fee
   f. Attach all necessary documents

OKLAHOMA

Step-1: Name Your Nonprofit

The name of your nonprofit will establish its brand and will allow you to incorporate with the state. The name you choose cannot conflict with any other organization registered within the state of Oklahoma. Make sure the name you choose is available and meets all state requirement. Search through the Oklahoma Secretary of State - Business Filing Department.

Step-2: Get Initial Directors and Incorporators

The incorporate is the individual who signs the Articles of Incorporation for your business. You will need at least one incorporator, but you can have additional. The directors are the governing body of your nonprofit and are stakeholders in the purpose and success of your nonprofit. You should have at least three directors who are unrelated individuals in order to meet IRS requirements. You'll also want to meet age and residency requirements.

Step-3: Selected a Registered Agent

The registered agent is responsible for receiving legal notices for your nonprofit. A registered agent needs to be physically living in the state and maintain an office open during regular business hours.

Step-4: Articles of Incorporation

The articles of incorporation are the official creation of your nonprofit. They show where and when the nonprofit was formed and provide the necessary information to verify the

nonprofits existence. Make sure your articles of incorporation meet state and IRS requirement.

Form: Certificate of Incorporation
Submit To: Oklahoma Secretary of State - Business Filing Department
How to File: Mail, fax, in person or online
Cost: $25
Time Frame: About 7-10 days by mail. About 1 day online.

Step-5: Get an Employer Identification Number (EIN)

This is a unique nine-digit number that the IRS assigned to identify your nonprofit. Your EIN is then used to open a bank account, apply for 501(c)(3) status and submit 990 IRS returns.

Form: IRS Form SS-4
Submit To: Internal Revenue Service (IRS)
How to File: Mail, phone, fax or online
Cost: $0
Time Frame: By phone or online is immediate, by fax is 4 days and by mail is 4-5 weeks.

Additional Notes:
- Print EIN before the closing session

Step-6: Storing Records

As you start a nonprofit, you will be faced with a number of official documents. Be sure you organize and store all of these records together for easy access later.

Step-7: Initial Governing Policies and Documents

The governing document for your nonprofit is your bylaws since they serve as the operating manual for your organization and need to be consistent with both the law and your articles of incorporation. The first meeting of your Board of Directors should be to review and ratify the bylaws.

You should also create and adopt a conflict of interest policy. This will guide you in what to do if someone in a key position within your nonprofit has competing interests and makes a decision that benefits themselves while harming your nonprofit. Organizational interests should be prioritized ahead of personal interests. All conflicts should be disclosed immediately.

Both the bylaws and the conflict of interest policy will need to be approved and adopted before applying to the IRS for 501(c)(3) status.

Step-8: Board of Directors Organizational Meeting

This initial meeting is the most productive and important one. You will approve bylaws, adopt the conflict of interest policy, elect directors, appoint officers and approve any resolutions like opening a bank account. Be sure to record the decisions made in meeting minutes.

Step-9: State Tax Identification Numbers and Accounts

Incorporating a nonprofit means, you will follow all state laws. Requirements vary by state so check with your individual state first.

To file in Oklahoma contact the Oklahoma Tax Commission.

Step-10: File for 501(c) Status

This can seem like one of the most difficult steps in starting your nonprofit, but it also offers many benefits. After applying and submitting your documents, the IRS will give you a Determination Letter that officially recognizes your tax-exempt status.

Form: IRS Form 1023, Form 1023-EZ or Form 1024
Submit To: Internal Revenue Service (IRS)
How to File: Mail
Cost: $275 for Form 1023-EZ and $600 for Form 1023
Time Frame: Less than a month for Form 1023-EZ and 3-6 months for Form 1023

Step-11: State Tax Exemption

Once you have your IRS Determination Letter, you next need to figure out your state's requirements for tax-exempt status. This is another area that varies by state. You may also need to do periodic renewals for tax-exempt status.

Oklahoma doesn't require filing for income tax exemption.

To file for Oklahoma sales tax exemption:
Form: 13-16-A: Application for Sales Tax Exemption
Submit To: Oklahoma Tax Commission
Cost: $0

Step-12: Charitable Solicitation Registration

This is yet another area where it varies between states, but most require it on an annual basis. This means you need to register with the state before fundraising from any resident of the state. Depending on the scope of your organization you may need to register in other states as well.

Overseen By: Oklahoma Secretary of State - Charitable Organizations Section

Exemptions:
1. Less than $10,000 charitable exemptions per year
2. Religious organizations
3. Educational institutions
4. Membership organizations
5. Appeals for individuals

To file in Oklahoma you need to do the following:

Form: SOS Form 101-01/13: Registration Statement of Charitable Organization
Submit To: Oklahoma Secretary of State - Charitable Organizations Section
How to File: Mail or online
Cost: $15-65 depending on contributions

Additional Notes:
- Attach all necessary documents
- Must be signed by the president, chairman or principal
- Doesn't need to be notarized

Step-13: Business Licenses and Permits

From here you will be all set to start your nonprofit. However, the work isn't over yet. You'll also need to stay in compliance with your nonprofit. Next, consider your required annual filings to remain legal.

Annual Renewal

1. IRS Renewals

a. IRS Form 990
   b. Due the 15th day of the 5th month following the end of the taxable year.
2. Oklahoma Corporate Tax Returns
   a. Filed with Oklahoma Secretary of State - Business Filing Department
   b. Form 512E: Oklahoma Return of Organization Exempt from Income Tax
   c. Costs $0
   d. Due four and a half months after the end of the fiscal year
3. Oklahoma has no renewal requirements for corporate income tax exemption.
4. Oklahoma has no renewal requirements for sales tax exemption.
5. Oklahoma has no annual report requirements.
6. Charitable Solicitation Renewal
   a. Filed with the Oklahoma Secretary of State - Charitable Organizations Section
   b. Form SOS Form 101-01/13: Registration Statement of Charitable Organization
   c. Filed by mail or online
   d. Costs $15-65 depending on contributions
   e. Due annually before the anniversary of your previous renewal
   f. Attach all necessary documents
   g. Must be signed by the president, chairman or principal
   h. Doesn't need to be notarized

OREGON

Step-1: Name Your Nonprofit

The name of your nonprofit will establish its brand and will allow you to incorporate with the state. The name you choose cannot conflict with any other organization registered within the state of Oregon. Make sure the name you choose is available and meets all state requirement. Search through the Oregon Secretary of State - Corporations Division.

Step-2: Get Initial Directors and Incorporators

The incorporate is the individual who signs the Articles of Incorporation for your business. You will need at least one incorporator, but you can have additional. The directors are the governing body of your nonprofit and are stakeholders in the purpose and success of your nonprofit. You should have at least three directors who are unrelated individuals in order to meet IRS requirements. You'll also want to meet age and residency requirements.

Step-3: Selected a Registered Agent

The registered agent is responsible for receiving legal notices for your nonprofit. A registered agent needs to be physically living in the state and maintain an office open during regular business hours.

Step-4: Articles of Incorporation

The articles of incorporation are the official creation of your nonprofit. They show where and when the nonprofit was formed and provide the necessary information to verify the nonprofits existence. Make sure your articles of incorporation meet state and IRS requirement.

Form: Articles of Incorporation

Submit To: Oregon Secretary of State - Corporations Division

How to File: Mail, fax, or online

Cost: $50

Time Frame: About 7-10 days by mail. About 1-2 days by fax. Instantly online.

Step-5: Get an Employer Identification Number (EIN)

This is a unique nine-digit number that the IRS assigned to identify your nonprofit. Your EIN is then used to open a bank account, apply for 501(c)(3) status and submit 990 IRS returns.

Form: IRS Form SS-4

Submit To: Internal Revenue Service (IRS)

How to File: Mail, phone, fax or online

Cost: $0

Time Frame: By phone or online is immediate, by fax is 4 days and by mail is 4-5 weeks.

Additional Notes:
- Print EIN before the closing session

Step-6: Storing Records

As you start a nonprofit, you will be faced with a number of official documents. Be sure you organize and store all of these records together for easy access later.

Step-7: Initial Governing Policies and Documents

The governing document for your nonprofit is your bylaws since they serve as the operating manual for your organization and need to be consistent with both the law and

your articles of incorporation. The first meeting of your Board of Directors should be to review and ratify the bylaws.

You should also create and adopt a conflict of interest policy. This will guide you in what to do if someone in a key position within your nonprofit has competing interests and makes a decision that benefits themselves while harming your nonprofit. Organizational interests should be prioritized ahead of personal interests. All conflicts should be disclosed immediately.

Both the bylaws and the conflict of interest policy will need to be approved and adopted before applying to the IRS for 501(c)(3) status.

Step-8: Board of Directors Organizational Meeting

This initial meeting is the most productive and important one. You will approve bylaws, adopt the conflict of interest policy, elect directors, appoint officers and approve any resolutions like opening a bank account. Be sure to record the decisions made in meeting minutes.

Step-9: State Tax Identification Numbers and Accounts

Incorporating a nonprofit means, you will follow all state laws. Requirements vary by state so check with your individual state first.

To file in Oregon contact the Oregon Department of Revenue.

Step-10: File for 501(c) Status

This can seem like one of the most difficult steps in starting your nonprofit, but it also offers many benefits. After applying and submitting your documents, the IRS will give you a Determination Letter that officially recognizes your tax-exempt status.

Form: IRS Form 1023, Form 1023-EZ or Form 1024
Submit To: Internal Revenue Service (IRS)
How to File: Mail
Cost: $275 for Form 1023-EZ and $600 for Form 1023
Time Frame: Less than a month for Form 1023-EZ and 3-6 months for Form 1023

Step-11: State Tax Exemption

Once you have your IRS Determination Letter, you next need to figure out your state's requirements for tax-exempt status. This is another area that varies by state. You may also need to do periodic renewals for tax-exempt status.

Oregon doesn't require filing for income tax exemption.

Oregon doesn't have a state-level sales tax.

Step-12: Charitable Solicitation Registration

This is yet another area where it varies between states, but most require it on an annual basis. This means you need to register with the state before fundraising from any resident of the state. Depending on the scope of your organization you may need to register in other states as well.

Overseen By: Oregon Department of Justice - Charitable Activities Section

Exemptions:

1. Unincorporated organizations
2. Religious organizations
3. Educational institutions
4. Mutual benefit corporations

To file in Oregon, you need to do the following:

Form: URS or Form RF-C: Registration for Charitable Organizations
Submit To: Oregon Department of Justice - Charitable Activities Section
How to File: Mail
Cost: $0

Additional Notes:
- Attach all necessary documents
- Must be signed by any officer or authorized representative
- Doesn't need to be notarized

Step-13: Business Licenses and Permits

From here you will be all set to start your nonprofit. However, the work isn't over yet. You'll also need to stay in compliance with your nonprofit. Next, consider your required annual filings to remain legal.

Annual Renewal

1. IRS Renewals
    a. IRS Form 990
    b. Due the 15th day of the 5th month following the end of the taxable year.
2. Oregon Corporate Tax Returns
    a. Filed with Oregon Department of Revenue

      b. Form 20 (Oregon Corporation Excise Tax Return)

      c. Due April 15th

3. Oregon has no renewal requirements for corporate income tax exemption.
4. Oregon has no renewal requirements for sales tax exemption.
5. Oregon requires the filing of an annual report
    a. Filed with Oregon Secretary of State - Corporations Division
    b. Filed online
    c. Costs $50
    d. Due annually by your registration anniversary date
    e. May be filed by anyone with authority
    f. Doesn't need original signatures
6. Charitable Solicitation Renewal
    a. Filed with the Oregon Department of Justice - Charitable Activities Section
    b. Form CT-12
    c. Filed by mail
    d. Costs $10-200 depending on contributions
    e. Due annually four and a half months after the fiscal year ends
    f. Attach all necessary documents

PENNSYLVANIA

Step-1: Name Your Nonprofit

The name of your nonprofit will establish its brand and will allow you to incorporate with the state. The name you choose cannot conflict with any other organization registered within the state of Pennsylvania. Make sure the name you choose is available and meets all state requirement. Search through the Pennsylvania Department of State - Bureau of Corporations and Charitable Organizations.

Step-2: Get Initial Directors and Incorporators

The incorporate is the individual who signs the Articles of Incorporation for your business. You will need at least one incorporator, but you can have additional. The directors are the governing body of your nonprofit and are stakeholders in the purpose and success of your nonprofit. You should have at least three directors who are unrelated individuals in order to meet IRS requirements. You'll also want to meet age and residency requirements.

Step-3: Selected a Registered Agent

The registered agent is responsible for receiving legal notices for your nonprofit. A registered agent needs to be physically living in the state and maintain an office open during regular business hours.

Step-4: Articles of Incorporation

The articles of incorporation are the official creation of your nonprofit. They show where and when the nonprofit was formed and provide the necessary information to verify the

nonprofits existence. Make sure your articles of incorporation meet state and IRS requirement.

Form: Articles of Incorporation
Submit To: Pennsylvania Department of State - Bureau of Corporations and Charitable Organizations
How to File: Mail or online
Cost: $125
Time Frame: About 5-10 days.

Step-5: Publish Incorporation
Pennsylvania nonprofits must publish filing articles of incorporation in two newspaper of general circulation, one of which is a legal newspaper. Both publications need to be in the county of your registered agent.

Step-6: Get an Employer Identification Number (EIN)

This is a unique nine-digit number that the IRS assigned to identify your nonprofit. Your EIN is then used to open a bank account, apply for 501(c)(3) status and submit 990 IRS returns.

Form: IRS Form SS-4
Submit To: Internal Revenue Service (IRS)
How to File: Mail, phone, fax or online
Cost: $0
Time Frame: By phone or online is immediate, by fax is 4 days and by mail is 4-5 weeks.

Additional Notes:
- Print EIN before the closing session

Step-7: Storing Records

As you start a nonprofit, you will be faced with a number of official documents. Be sure you organize and store all of these records together for easy access later.

Step-8: Initial Governing Policies and Documents

The governing document for your nonprofit is your bylaws since they serve as the operating manual for your organization and need to be consistent with both the law and your articles of incorporation. The first meeting of your Board of Directors should be to review and ratify the bylaws.

You should also create and adopt a conflict of interest policy. This will guide you in what to do if someone in a key position within your nonprofit has competing interests and makes a decision that benefits themselves while harming your nonprofit. Organizational interests should be prioritized ahead of personal interests. All conflicts should be disclosed immediately.

Both the bylaws and the conflict of interest policy will need to be approved and adopted before applying to the IRS for 501(c)(3) status.

Step-9: Board of Directors Organizational Meeting

This initial meeting is the most productive and important one. You will approve bylaws, adopt the conflict of interest policy, elect directors, appoint officers and approve any resolutions like opening a bank account. Be sure to record the decisions made in meeting minutes.

Step-10: State Tax Identification Numbers and Accounts

Incorporating a nonprofit means, you will follow all state laws. Requirements vary by state so check with your individual state first.

To file in Pennsylvania:

Form: PA-100: PA Enterprise Registration Form
Submit To: Pennsylvania Department of Revenue
How to File: Mail or online
Cost: $0

Step-11: File for 501(c) Status

This can seem like one of the most difficult steps in starting your nonprofit, but it also offers many benefits. After applying and submitting your documents, the IRS will give you a Determination Letter that officially recognizes your tax-exempt status.

Form: IRS Form 1023, Form 1023-EZ or Form 1024
Submit To: Internal Revenue Service (IRS)
How to File: Mail
Cost: $275 for Form 1023-EZ and $600 for Form 1023
Time Frame: Less than a month for Form 1023-EZ and 3-6 months for Form 1023

Step-12: State Tax Exemption

Once you have your IRS Determination Letter, you next need to figure out your state's requirements for tax-exempt status. This is another area that varies by state. You may also need to do periodic renewals for tax-exempt status.

Pennsylvania doesn't require filing for income tax exemption.

For Pennsylvania sales tax exemption:

Form: REV-72: Application for Sales Tax Exemption
Submit To: Pennsylvania Department of Revenue
Cost: $0
Due: Once every 5 years about 2 months before expiration

Step-13: Charitable Solicitation Registration

This is yet another area where it varies between states, but most require it on an annual basis. This means you need to register with the state before fundraising from any resident of the state. Depending on the scope of your organization you may need to register in other states as well.

Overseen By: Pennsylvania Department of State - Bureau of Charitable Organizations

Exemptions:
1. Less than $25,000 gross annual national contributions
2. Religious organizations
3. Educational institutions
4. PTAs
5. Public safety organizations
6. Hospitals
7. Library organizations

To file in Pennsylvania, you need to do the following:

Form: BCO-10: Charitable Organization Registration Statement
Submit To: Pennsylvania Department of State - Bureau of Charitable Organizations
How to File: Mail
Cost: $15-250 depending on contributions

Additional Notes:
- Attach all necessary documents

Step-14: Business Licenses and Permits

From here you will be all set to start your nonprofit. However, the work isn't over yet. You'll also need to stay in compliance with your nonprofit. Next, consider your required annual filings to remain legal.

Annual Renewal

1. IRS Renewals
    a. IRS Form 990
    b. Due the 15th day of the 5th month following the end of the taxable year
2. Pennsylvania has no renewal requirements for corporate income tax exemption.
3. To renew sales tax exemption in Pennsylvania
    a. Filed with Pennsylvania Department of Revenue
    b. Form REV-72: Application for Sales Tax Exemption
    c. Costs $0
    d. Due every 5 years
4. Pennsylvania requires the filing of an annual report
    a. Filed with Pennsylvania Department of State - Bureau of Corporations and Charitable Organizations
    b. Filed by mail or online
    c. Costs $0
    d. Due by April 30th of each year when there is a change in the organization the previous year
5. Charitable Solicitation Renewal
    a. Filed with the Pennsylvania Department of State - Bureau of Corporation and Charitable Organizations
    b. Form BCO-10: Charitable Organization Registration Statement

c. Filed by mail
d. Costs $15-250 depending on contributions
e. Due annually ten and a half months after fiscal year ends
f. You must attach an annual financial report

RHODE ISLAND

Step-1: Name Your Nonprofit

The name of your nonprofit will establish its brand and will allow you to incorporate with the state. The name you choose cannot conflict with any other organization registered within the state of Rhode Island. Make sure the name you choose is available and meets all state requirement. Search through the Rhode Island Secretary of State.

Step-2: Get Initial Directors and Incorporators

The incorporate is the individual who signs the Articles of Incorporation for your business. You will need at least one incorporator, but you can have additional. The directors are the governing body of your nonprofit and are stakeholders in the purpose and success of your nonprofit. You should have at least three directors who are unrelated individuals in order to meet IRS requirements. You'll also want to meet age and residency requirements.

Step-3: Selected a Registered Agent

The registered agent is responsible for receiving legal notices for your nonprofit. A registered agent needs to be physically living in the state and maintain an office open during regular business hours.

Step-4: Articles of Incorporation

The articles of incorporation are the official creation of your nonprofit. They show where and when the nonprofit was formed and provide the necessary information to verify the nonprofits existence. Make sure your articles of incorporation meet state and IRS requirement.

Form: Form 200: Articles of Incorporation
Submit To: Rhode Island Secretary of State
How to File: Mail, in person or online
Cost: $35
Time Frame: About 7 days by mail or online. Same day for filing in person.

Step-5: Get an Employer Identification Number (EIN)

This is a unique nine-digit number that the IRS assigned to identify your nonprofit. Your EIN is then used to open a bank account, apply for 501(c)(3) status and submit 990 IRS returns.

Form: IRS Form SS-4
Submit To: Internal Revenue Service (IRS)
How to File: Mail, phone, fax or online
Cost: $0
Time Frame: By phone or online is immediate, by fax is 4 days and by mail is 4-5 weeks.

Additional Notes:
- Print EIN before the closing session

Step-6: Storing Records

As you start a nonprofit, you will be faced with a number of official documents. Be sure you organize and store all of these records together for easy access later.

Step-7: Initial Governing Policies and Documents

The governing document for your nonprofit is your bylaws since they serve as the operating manual for your organization and need to be consistent with both the law and

your articles of incorporation. The first meeting of your Board of Directors should be to review and ratify the bylaws.

You should also create and adopt a conflict of interest policy. This will guide you in what to do if someone in a key position within your nonprofit has competing interests and makes a decision that benefits themselves while harming your nonprofit. Organizational interests should be prioritized ahead of personal interests. All conflicts should be disclosed immediately.

Both the bylaws and the conflict of interest policy will need to be approved and adopted before applying to the IRS for 501(c)(3) status.

Step-8: Board of Directors Organizational Meeting

This initial meeting is the most productive and important one. You will approve bylaws, adopt the conflict of interest policy, elect directors, appoint officers and approve any resolutions like opening a bank account. Be sure to record the decisions made in meeting minutes.

Step-9: State Tax Identification Numbers and Accounts

Incorporating a nonprofit means, you will follow all state laws. Requirements vary by state so check with your individual state first.

To file in Rhode Island:

Form: BAR: Business Application and Registration
Submit To: State of Rhode Island: Division of Taxation
How to File: Mail or online
Cost: Varies based on licenses/permits

Step-10: File for 501(c) Status

This can seem like one of the most difficult steps in starting your nonprofit, but it also offers many benefits. After applying and submitting your documents, the IRS will give you a Determination Letter that officially recognizes your tax-exempt status.

Form: IRS Form 1023, Form 1023-EZ or Form 1024
Submit To: Internal Revenue Service (IRS)
How to File: Mail
Cost: $275 for Form 1023-EZ and $600 for Form 1023
Time Frame: Less than a month for Form 1023-EZ and 3-6 months for Form 1023

Step-11: State Tax Exemption

Once you have your IRS Determination Letter, you next need to figure out your state's requirements for tax-exempt status. This is another area that varies by state. You may also need to do periodic renewals for tax-exempt status.

Rhode Island doesn't require filing for income tax exemption.

For Rhode Island sales tax exemption:

Form: EXO-APP: Application for Exemption for an Exempt Organization
Submit To: Rhode Island Department of Revenue - Division of Taxation
Cost: $25

Step-12: Charitable Solicitation Registration

This is yet another area where it varies between states, but most require it on an annual basis. This means you need to register with the state before fundraising from any

resident of the state. Depending on the scope of your organization you may need to register in other states as well.

Overseen By: Rhode Island Department of Business Registration

Exemptions:
1. Less than $25,000 per fiscal year
2. Religious organizations
3. Educational institutions
4. Appeals for named individuals
5. Membership organizations
6. Foundations

To file in Rhode Island, you need to do the following:

Form: Charitable Organizations Application
Submit To: Rhode Island Department of Business Regulation
How to File: Online
Cost: $90

Additional Notes:
- Attach all necessary documents

Step-13: Business Licenses and Permits
From here you will be all set to start your nonprofit. However, the work isn't over yet. You'll also need to stay in compliance with your nonprofit. Next, consider your required annual filings to remain legal.

Annual Renewal

1. IRS Renewals
   a. IRS Form 990
   b. Due the 15th day of the 5th month following the end of the taxable year
2. Rhode Island Corporate Tax Returns
   a. Filed with Rhode Island Department of Revenue - Division of Taxation
   b. Form RI-1120C
   c. Due three and a half months after the fiscal year ends
3. Rhode Island has no renewal requirements for corporate income tax exemption.
4. Rhode Island has no renewal requirements for sales tax exemption.
5. Rhode Island requires the filing of an annual report
   a. Filed with Rhode Island Secretary of State
   b. Form 631: Nonprofit Corporation Annual Report
   c. Filed by mail or online
   d. Costs $20
   e. Due by June 30th
   f. $25 late fee
   g. May be filed by anyone with authority
   h. Doesn't need original signatures
6. Charitable Solicitation Renewal
   a. Filed with the Rhode Island Department of Business Regulation
   b. Form Charitable Organizations Application
   c. Filed online
   d. Costs $90
   e. Due annually by the anniversary of initial registration
   f. You must attach an annual financial report

SOUTH CAROLINA

Step-1: Name Your Nonprofit

The name of your nonprofit will establish its brand and will allow you to incorporate with the state. The name you choose cannot conflict with any other organization registered within the state of South Carolina. Make sure the name you choose is available and meets all state requirement. Search through the South Carolina Secretary of State - Division of Business Filings.

Step-2: Get Initial Directors and Incorporators

The incorporate is the individual who signs the Articles of Incorporation for your business. You will need at least one incorporator, but you can have additional. The directors are the governing body of your nonprofit and are stakeholders in the purpose and success of your nonprofit. You should have at least three directors who are unrelated individuals in order to meet IRS requirements. You'll also want to meet age and residency requirements.

Step-3: Selected a Registered Agent

The registered agent is responsible for receiving legal notices for your nonprofit. A registered agent needs to be physically living in the state and maintain an office open during regular business hours.

Step-4: Articles of Incorporation

The articles of incorporation are the official creation of your nonprofit. They show where and when the nonprofit was formed and provide the necessary information to verify the

nonprofits existence. Make sure your articles of incorporation meet state and IRS requirement.

Form: Articles of Incorporations
Submit To: South Carolina Secretary of State - Division of Business Filings
How to File: Mail or online
Cost: $25
Time Frame: About 7-10 days by mail. About 1-2 days online.

Additional Notes:
- Submit the original and a copy
- Include a self-addressed stamped envelope

Step-5: Get an Employer Identification Number (EIN)

This is a unique nine-digit number that the IRS assigned to identify your nonprofit. Your EIN is then used to open a bank account, apply for 501(c)(3) status and submit 990 IRS returns.

Form: IRS Form SS-4
Submit To: Internal Revenue Service (IRS)
How to File: Mail, phone, fax or online
Cost: $0
Time Frame: By phone or online is immediate, by fax is 4 days and by mail is 4-5 weeks.

Additional Notes:
- Print EIN before the closing session

Step-6: Storing Records

As you start a nonprofit, you will be faced with a number of official documents. Be sure you organize and store all of these records together for easy access later.

Step-7: Initial Governing Policies and Documents

The governing document for your nonprofit is your bylaws since they serve as the operating manual for your organization and need to be consistent with both the law and your articles of incorporation. The first meeting of your Board of Directors should be to review and ratify the bylaws.

You should also create and adopt a conflict of interest policy. This will guide you in what to do if someone in a key position within your nonprofit has competing interests and makes a decision that benefits themselves while harming your nonprofit. Organizational interests should be prioritized ahead of personal interests. All conflicts should be disclosed immediately.

Both the bylaws and the conflict of interest policy will need to be approved and adopted before applying to the IRS for 501(c)(3) status.

Step-8: Board of Directors Organizational Meeting
This initial meeting is the most productive and important one. You will approve bylaws, adopt the conflict of interest policy, elect directors, appoint officers and approve any resolutions like opening a bank account. Be sure to record the decisions made in meeting minutes.

Step-9: State Tax Identification Numbers and Accounts

Incorporating a nonprofit means, you will follow all state laws. Requirements vary by state so check with your individual state first.

To file in South Carolina:

Form: SCDOR-111: South Carolina Department of Revenue Tax Registration Application
Submit To: South Carolina Department of Revenue
How to File: Mail or online
Cost: Varies based on licenses/permits

Step-10: File for 501(c) Status

This can seem like one of the most difficult steps in starting your nonprofit, but it also offers many benefits. After applying and submitting your documents, the IRS will give you a Determination Letter that officially recognizes your tax-exempt status.

Form: IRS Form 1023, Form 1023-EZ or Form 1024
Submit To: Internal Revenue Service (IRS)
How to File: Mail
Cost: $275 for Form 1023-EZ and $600 for Form 1023
Time Frame: Less than a month for Form 1023-EZ and 3-6 months for Form 1023

Step-11: State Tax Exemption

Once you have your IRS Determination Letter, you next need to figure out your state's requirements for tax-exempt status. This is another area that varies by state. You may also need to do periodic renewals for tax-exempt status.

South Carolina doesn't require filing for income tax exemption.

For South Carolina sales tax exemption:
Form: ST-387: Application for Sales Tax Exemption

Submit To: South Carolina Department of Revenue

Cost: $0

Step-12: Charitable Solicitation Registration

This is yet another area where it varies between states, but most require it on an annual basis. This means you need to register with the state before fundraising from any resident of the state. Depending on the scope of your organization you may need to register in other states as well.

Overseen By: South Carolina Secretary of State - Division of Public Charities

Exemptions:
1. Less than $7,500 per the calendar year
2. Religious organizations
3. Educational institutions
4. Appeals for named individuals
5. Political groups and individuals

To file in South Carolina, you need to do the following:

Form: Registration Statement for a Charitable Organization
Submit To: South Carolina Secretary of State - Division of Public Charities
How to File: Mail or online
Cost: $50

Additional Notes:
- Must be signed by CEO and CFO
- Attach all documents

Step-13: Business Licenses and Permits

From here you will be all set to start your nonprofit. However, the work isn't over yet. You'll also need to stay in compliance with your nonprofit. Next, consider your required annual filings to remain legal.

Annual Renewal

1. IRS Renewals
    a. IRS Form 990
    b. Due the 15th day of the 5th month following the end of the taxable year
2. South Carolina Corporate Tax Returns
    a. Filed with South Carolina Department of Revenue
    b. Form SC 990-T
    c. File by mail
    d. Due annually by the 15th day of the 5th month at the end of the tax year
3. South Carolina has no renewal requirements for corporate income tax exemption.
4. South Carolina has no renewal requirements for sales tax exemption.
5. South Carolina doesn't require an annual report
6. Charitable Solicitation Renewal
    a. Filed with the South Carolina Secretary of State - Division of Public Charities
    b. Form Registration Statement for a Charitable Organization or Application for Registration Exemption
    c. Filed by mail or online
    d. Costs $50
    e. Due annually four and a half months after the end of the fiscal year
    f. Must be signed by the CEO and CFO
    g. Must submit with a financial statement

SOUTH DAKOTA

Step-1: Name Your Nonprofit

The name of your nonprofit will establish its brand and will allow you to incorporate with the state. The name you choose cannot conflict with any other organization registered within the state of South Dakota. Make sure the name you choose is available and meets all state requirement. Search through the South Dakota Secretary of State.

Step-2: Get Initial Directors and Incorporators

The incorporate is the individual who signs the Articles of Incorporation for your business. You will need at least one incorporator, but you can have additional. The directors are the governing body of your nonprofit and are stakeholders in the purpose and success of your nonprofit. You should have at least three directors who are unrelated individuals in order to meet IRS requirements. You'll also want to meet age and residency requirements.

Step-3: Selected a Registered Agent

The registered agent is responsible for receiving legal notices for your nonprofit. A registered agent needs to be physically living in the state and maintain an office open during regular business hours.

Step-4: Articles of Incorporation

The articles of incorporation are the official creation of your nonprofit. They show where and when the nonprofit was formed and provide the necessary information to verify the nonprofits existence. Make sure your articles of incorporation meet state and IRS requirement.

Form: Articles of Incorporations
Submit To: South Dakota Secretary of State
How to File: Mail
Cost: $30. Optional $50 expedite.
Time Frame: About 3-5 days.

Additional Notes:
- Submit an original and a copy

Step-5: Get an Employer Identification Number (EIN)

This is a unique nine-digit number that the IRS assigned to identify your nonprofit. Your EIN is then used to open a bank account, apply for 501(c)(3) status and submit 990 IRS returns.

Form: IRS Form SS-4
Submit To: Internal Revenue Service (IRS)
How to File: Mail, phone, fax or online
Cost: $0
Time Frame: By phone or online is immediate, by fax is 4 days and by mail is 4-5 weeks.

Additional Notes:
- Print EIN before the closing session

Step-6: Storing Records

As you start a nonprofit, you will be faced with a number of official documents. Be sure you organize and store all of these records together for easy access later.

Step-7: Initial Governing Policies and Documents

The governing document for your nonprofit is your bylaws since they serve as the operating manual for your organization and need to be consistent with both the law and your articles of incorporation. The first meeting of your Board of Directors should be to review and ratify the bylaws.

You should also create and adopt a conflict of interest policy. This will guide you in what to do if someone in a key position within your nonprofit has competing interests and makes a decision that benefits themselves while harming your nonprofit. Organizational interests should be prioritized ahead of personal interests. All conflicts should be disclosed immediately.

Both the bylaws and the conflict of interest policy will need to be approved and adopted before applying to the IRS for 501(c)(3) status.

Step-8: Board of Directors Organizational Meeting

This initial meeting is the most productive and important one. You will approve bylaws, adopt the conflict of interest policy, elect directors, appoint officers and approve any resolutions like opening a bank account. Be sure to record the decisions made in meeting minutes.

Step-9: State Tax Identification Numbers and Accounts

Incorporating a nonprofit means, you will follow all state laws. Requirements vary by state so check with your individual state first.
To file in South Dakota:

Form: South Dakota Tax License Application
Submit To: South Dakota Department of Revenue
How to File: Online

Cost: Varies based on licenses/permits

Step-10: File for 501(c) Status

This can seem like one of the most difficult steps in starting your nonprofit, but it also offers many benefits. After applying and submitting your documents, the IRS will give you a Determination Letter that officially recognizes your tax-exempt status.

Form: IRS Form 1023, Form 1023-EZ or Form 1024
Submit To: Internal Revenue Service (IRS)
How to File: Mail
Cost: $275 for Form 1023-EZ and $600 for Form 1023
Time Frame: Less than a month for Form 1023-EZ and 3-6 months for Form 1023

Step-11: State Tax Exemption

Once you have your IRS Determination Letter, you next need to figure out your state's requirements for tax-exempt status. This is another area that varies by state. You may also need to do periodic renewals for tax-exempt status.

South Dakota doesn't require filing for income tax exemption.

For South Dakota sales tax exemption:

Form: Sales Tax Exempt Status Application
Submit To: South Dakota Department of Revenue
Cost: $0

Step-12: Charitable Solicitation Registration

This is yet another area where it varies between states, but most require it on an annual basis. This means you need to register with the state before fundraising from any resident of the state. Depending on the scope of your organization you may need to register in other states as well.

South Dakota doesn't require registering for this.

Step-13: Business Licenses and Permits

From here you will be all set to start your nonprofit. However, the work isn't over yet. You'll also need to stay in compliance with your nonprofit. Next, consider your required annual filings to remain legal.

Annual Renewal

1. IRS Renewals
    a. IRS Form 990
    b. Due the 15th day of the 5th month following the end of the taxable year
2. South Dakota has no renewal requirements for corporate income tax exemption.
3. To renew sales tax exemption in South Dakota
    a. Filed with South Dakota Department of Revenue
    b. Sales Tax Exempt Status Application
    c. Costs $0
    d. Due every 5 years
4. South Dakota requires the filing of an annual report
    a. Filed with South Dakota Secretary of State
    b. Form Annual Report Domestic Nonprofit Corporations
    c. Filed by mail or online
    d. Costs $10
    e. Return in about a week

f. Due by the first day of the registration anniversary month
g. May be filed by anyone with authority
h. Doesn't need original signatures

TENNESSEE

Step-1: Name Your Nonprofit

The name of your nonprofit will establish its brand and will allow you to incorporate with the state. The name you choose cannot conflict with any other organization registered within the state of Tennessee. Make sure the name you choose is available and meets all state requirement. Search through the Tennessee Secretary of State - Division of Business Services.

Step-2: Get Initial Directors and Incorporators

The incorporate is the individual who signs the Articles of Incorporation for your business. You will need at least one incorporator, but you can have additional. The directors are the governing body of your nonprofit and are stakeholders in the purpose and success of your nonprofit. You should have at least three directors who are unrelated individuals in order to meet IRS requirements. You'll also want to meet age and residency requirements.

Step-3: Selected a Registered Agent

The registered agent is responsible for receiving legal notices for your nonprofit. A registered agent needs to be physically living in the state and maintain an office open during regular business hours.

Step-4: Articles of Incorporation

The articles of incorporation are the official creation of your nonprofit. They show where and when the nonprofit was formed and provide the necessary information to verify the

nonprofits existence. Make sure your articles of incorporation meet state and IRS requirement.

Form: Charter (ss-4418)
Submit To: Tennessee Secretary of State - Division of Business Services
How to File: Online
Cost: $100
Time Frame: About 4 days by mail. About 2 days online. Immediately in person.

Step-5: Get an Employer Identification Number (EIN)

This is a unique nine-digit number that the IRS assigned to identify your nonprofit. Your EIN is then used to open a bank account, apply for 501(c)(3) status and submit 990 IRS returns.

Form: IRS Form SS-4
Submit To: Internal Revenue Service (IRS)
How to File: Mail, phone, fax or online
Cost: $0
Time Frame: By phone or online is immediate, by fax is 4 days and by mail is 4-5 weeks.

Additional Notes:
- Print EIN before the closing session

Step-6: Storing Records

As you start a nonprofit, you will be faced with a number of official documents. Be sure you organize and store all of these records together for easy access later.

Step-7: Initial Governing Policies and Documents

The governing document for your nonprofit is your bylaws since they serve as the operating manual for your organization and need to be consistent with both the law and your articles of incorporation. The first meeting of your Board of Directors should be to review and ratify the bylaws.

You should also create and adopt a conflict of interest policy. This will guide you in what to do if someone in a key position within your nonprofit has competing interests and makes a decision that benefits themselves while harming your nonprofit. Organizational interests should be prioritized ahead of personal interests. All conflicts should be disclosed immediately.

Both the bylaws and the conflict of interest policy will need to be approved and adopted before applying to the IRS for 501(c)(3) status.

Step-8: Board of Directors Organizational Meeting

This initial meeting is the most productive and important one. You will approve bylaws, adopt the conflict of interest policy, elect directors, appoint officers and approve any resolutions like opening a bank account. Be sure to record the decisions made in meeting minutes.

Step-9: State Tax Identification Numbers and Accounts

Incorporating a nonprofit means, you will follow all state laws. Requirements vary by state so check with your individual state first.

To file in Tennessee:

Form: RV-F1300501: Tennessee Department of Revenue Application for Registration
Submit To: Tennessee Department of Revenue

How to File: Mail or online
Cost: $0

Step-10: File for 501(c) Status

This can seem like one of the most difficult steps in starting your nonprofit, but it also offers many benefits. After applying and submitting your documents, the IRS will give you a Determination Letter that officially recognizes your tax-exempt status.

Form: IRS Form 1023, Form 1023-EZ or Form 1024
Submit To: Internal Revenue Service (IRS)
How to File: Mail
Cost: $275 for Form 1023-EZ and $600 for Form 1023
Time Frame: Less than a month for Form 1023-EZ and 3-6 months for Form 1023

Step-11: State Tax Exemption

Once you have your IRS Determination Letter, you next need to figure out your state's requirements for tax-exempt status. This is another area that varies by state. You may also need to do periodic renewals for tax-exempt status.

Tennessee doesn't require filing for income tax exemption.

For South Dakota sales tax exemption:

Form: RV-F1306901: Application for Registration - Sales and Use Tax Exempt Entities
Submit To: Tennessee Department of Revenue
Cost: $0
Step-12: Charitable Solicitation Registration

This is yet another area where it varies between states, but most require it on an annual basis. This means you need to register with the state before fundraising from any resident of the state. Depending on the scope of your organization you may need to register in other states as well.

Overseen By: Tennessee Secretary of State - Division of Charitable Solicitations and Gaming.

Exemptions:
1. Less than $30,000 contributions per the calendar year
2. Religious organizations
3. Educational institutions

To file in Tennessee, you need to do the following:

Form: SS-6001: Application for Registration of a Charitable Organization
Submit To: Tennessee Secretary of State - Division of Charitable Solicitations and Gaming
How to File: Mail or online
Cost: $50

Additional Notes:
- Attach all necessary documents
- Must be signed by the CFO and another officer
- Signatures don't need to be notarized

Step-13: Business Licenses and Permits
From here you will be all set to start your nonprofit. However, the work isn't over yet. You'll also need to stay in compliance with your nonprofit. Next, consider your required annual filings to remain legal.

Annual Renewal

1. IRS Renewals
   a. IRS Form 990
   b. Due the 15th day of the 5th month following the end of the taxable year
2. Tennessee has no renewal requirements for corporate income tax exemption.
3. Tennessee has no renewal requirements for sales tax exemption.
4. Tennessee requires the filing of an annual report
   a. Filed with Tennessee Secretary of State - Division of Business Services
   b. Filed by mail or online
   c. Costs $20. Optional $2.25 online filing fee.
   d. Due by the first day of the fourth month after the end of the fiscal year
   e. May be filed by an authorized officer, member or partner
   f. Doesn't need original signatures
5. Charitable Solicitation Renewal
   a. Filed with the Tennessee Secretary of State - Division of Charitable Solicitations and Gaming
   b. Form SS-6002: Application to Renew Registration of a Charitable Organization
   c. Filed by mail or online
   d. Costs $80-240 depending on gross revenue
   e. Renewal is annually within 6 months after the end of the fiscal year
   f. Must be signed by the CFO and another officer
   g. Signatures don't need to be notarized

TEXAS

Step-1: Name Your Nonprofit

The name of your nonprofit will establish its brand and will allow you to incorporate with the state. The name you choose cannot conflict with any other organization registered within the state of Texas. Make sure the name you choose is available and meets all state requirement. Search through the Texas Secretary of State - Corporations Section.

Step-2: Get Initial Directors and Incorporators

The incorporate is the individual who signs the Articles of Incorporation for your business. You will need at least one incorporator, but you can have additional. The directors are the governing body of your nonprofit and are stakeholders in the purpose and success of your nonprofit. You should have at least three directors who are unrelated individuals in order to meet IRS requirements. You'll also want to meet age and residency requirements.

Step-3: Selected a Registered Agent

The registered agent is responsible for receiving legal notices for your nonprofit. A registered agent needs to be physically living in the state and maintain an office open during regular business hours.

Step-4: Articles of Incorporation

The articles of incorporation are the official creation of your nonprofit. They show where and when the nonprofit was formed and provide the necessary information to verify the nonprofits existence. Make sure your articles of incorporation meet state and IRS requirement.

Form: 202: Certificate of Formation for a Nonprofit Corporation

Submit To: Texas Secretary of State - Corporations Section

How to File: Mail, fax or in person

Cost: $25

Time Frame: About 3-5 days by mail or fax

Additional Notes:
- Submit an original and a copy

Step-5: Get an Employer Identification Number (EIN)

This is a unique nine-digit number that the IRS assigned to identify your nonprofit. Your EIN is then used to open a bank account, apply for 501(c)(3) status and submit 990 IRS returns.

Form: IRS Form SS-4

Submit To: Internal Revenue Service (IRS)

How to File: Mail, phone, fax or online

Cost: $0

Time Frame: By phone or online is immediate, by fax is 4 days and by mail is 4-5 weeks.

Additional Notes:
- Print EIN before the closing session

Step-6: Storing Records

As you start a nonprofit, you will be faced with a number of official documents. Be sure you organize and store all of these records together for easy access later.

Step-7: Initial Governing Policies and Documents

The governing document for your nonprofit is your bylaws since they serve as the operating manual for your organization and need to be consistent with both the law and your articles of incorporation. The first meeting of your Board of Directors should be to review and ratify the bylaws.

You should also create and adopt a conflict of interest policy. This will guide you in what to do if someone in a key position within your nonprofit has competing interests and makes a decision that benefits themselves while harming your nonprofit. Organizational interests should be prioritized ahead of personal interests. All conflicts should be disclosed immediately.

Both the bylaws and the conflict of interest policy will need to be approved and adopted before applying to the IRS for 501(c)(3) status.

Step-8: Board of Directors Organizational Meeting

This initial meeting is the most productive and important one. You will approve bylaws, adopt the conflict of interest policy, elect directors, appoint officers and approve any resolutions like opening a bank account. Be sure to record the decisions made in meeting minutes.

Step-9: State Tax Identification Numbers and Accounts

Incorporating a nonprofit means, you will follow all state laws. Requirements vary by state so check with your individual state first.
To file in Texas:

Form: Texas Tax Forms
Submit To: Texas Taxes - Texas Comptroller of Public Accounts
How to File: Mail or online

Cost: Varies

Step-10: File for 501(c) Status

This can seem like one of the most difficult steps in starting your nonprofit, but it also offers many benefits. After applying and submitting your documents, the IRS will give you a Determination Letter that officially recognizes your tax-exempt status.

Form: IRS Form 1023, Form 1023-EZ or Form 1024
Submit To: Internal Revenue Service (IRS)
How to File: Mail
Cost: $275 for Form 1023-EZ and $600 for Form 1023
Time Frame: Less than a month for Form 1023-EZ and 3-6 months for Form 1023

Step-11: State Tax Exemption

Once you have your IRS Determination Letter, you next need to figure out your state's requirements for tax-exempt status. This is another area that varies by state. You may also need to do periodic renewals for tax-exempt status.

For Texas income tax exemption:

Form: AP-204, AP-205, AP-206, AP-207 and AP-209
Submit To: Texas Comptroller
Cost: $0

For Texas sales tax exemption:

Form: AP-205-2: Application for Exemption - Charitable Organizations
Submit To: Texas Comptroller
Cost: $0

Step-12: Charitable Solicitation Registration

This is yet another area where it varies between states, but most require it on an annual basis. This means you need to register with the state before fundraising from any resident of the state. Depending on the scope of your organization you may need to register in other states as well.

Overseen By: Texas Secretary of State - Registration Unit

Exemptions: None

Contact for specifics

Step-13: Business Licenses and Permits

From here you will be all set to start your nonprofit. However, the work isn't over yet. You'll also need to stay in compliance with your nonprofit. Next, consider your required annual filings to remain legal.

Annual Renewal

1. IRS Renewals
    a. IRS Form 990
    b. Due the 15th day of the 5th month following the end of the taxable year
2. Texas has no renewal requirements for corporate income tax exemption.
3. Texas has no renewal requirements for sales tax exemption.
4. Texas requires the filing of a public information report
    a. Filed with the Texas Comptroller
    b. Form Public Information Report
    c. Filed by mail

      d. Costs $0

      e. Due annually by May 15th

      f. File two copies

      g. Must be filed by an officer, director, manager, member, partner or agent

      h. Doesn't need original signatures

5. Charitable Solicitation Renewal

      a. Filed with the Texas Secretary of State - Registrations Unit

      b. Due annually by registration anniversary date

UTAH

Step-1: Name Your Nonprofit

The name of your nonprofit will establish its brand and will allow you to incorporate with the state. The name you choose cannot conflict with any other organization registered within the state of Utah. Make sure the name you choose is available and meets all state requirement. Search through the Utah Department of Commerce - Division of Corporations.

Step-2: Get Initial Directors and Incorporators

The incorporate is the individual who signs the Articles of Incorporation for your business. You will need at least one incorporator, but you can have additional. The directors are the governing body of your nonprofit and are stakeholders in the purpose and success of your nonprofit. You should have at least three directors who are unrelated individuals in order to meet IRS requirements. You'll also want to meet age and residency requirements.

Step-3: Selected a Registered Agent

The registered agent is responsible for receiving legal notices for your nonprofit. A registered agent needs to be physically living in the state and maintain an office open during regular business hours.

Step-4: Articles of Incorporation

The articles of incorporation are the official creation of your nonprofit. They show where and when the nonprofit was formed and provide the necessary information to verify the

nonprofits existence. Make sure your articles of incorporation meet state and IRS requirement.

Form: Articles of Incorporation
Submit To: Utah Department of Commerce - Division of Corporations
How to File: Mail, fax, in person or online
Cost: $30
Time Frame: About 14 days by mail or fax. About 1 day online.

Step-5: Get an Employer Identification Number (EIN)

This is a unique nine-digit number that the IRS assigned to identify your nonprofit. Your EIN is then used to open a bank account, apply for 501(c)(3) status and submit 990 IRS returns.

Form: IRS Form SS-4
Submit To: Internal Revenue Service (IRS)
How to File: Mail, phone, fax or online
Cost: $0
Time Frame: By phone or online is immediate, by fax is 4 days and by mail is 4-5 weeks.

Additional Notes:
- Print EIN before the closing session

Step-6: Storing Records

As you start a nonprofit, you will be faced with a number of official documents. Be sure you organize and store all of these records together for easy access later.

Step-7: Initial Governing Policies and Documents

The governing document for your nonprofit is your bylaws since they serve as the operating manual for your organization and need to be consistent with both the law and your articles of incorporation. The first meeting of your Board of Directors should be to review and ratify the bylaws.

You should also create and adopt a conflict of interest policy. This will guide you in what to do if someone in a key position within your nonprofit has competing interests and makes a decision that benefits themselves while harming your nonprofit. Organizational interests should be prioritized ahead of personal interests. All conflicts should be disclosed immediately.

Both the bylaws and the conflict of interest policy will need to be approved and adopted before applying to the IRS for 501(c)(3) status.

Step-8: Board of Directors Organizational Meeting

This initial meeting is the most productive and important one. You will approve bylaws, adopt the conflict of interest policy, elect directors, appoint officers and approve any resolutions like opening a bank account. Be sure to record the decisions made in meeting minutes.

Step-9: State Tax Identification Numbers and Accounts

Incorporating a nonprofit means, you will follow all state laws. Requirements vary by state so check with your individual state first.

To file in Utah:

Form: TC-69: Utah State Business and Tax Registration
Submit To: Utah State Tax Commission

How to File: Mail or online
Cost: $0

Step-10: File for 501(c) Status

This can seem like one of the most difficult steps in starting your nonprofit, but it also offers many benefits. After applying and submitting your documents, the IRS will give you a Determination Letter that officially recognizes your tax-exempt status.

Form: IRS Form 1023, Form 1023-EZ or Form 1024
Submit To: Internal Revenue Service (IRS)
How to File: Mail
Cost: $275 for Form 1023-EZ and $600 for Form 1023
Time Frame: Less than a month for Form 1023-EZ and 3-6 months for Form 1023

Step-11: State Tax Exemption

Once you have your IRS Determination Letter, you next need to figure out your state's requirements for tax-exempt status. This is another area that varies by state. You may also need to do periodic renewals for tax-exempt status.

For Utah income tax exemption:

Form: TC-161: Registration for Exemption from Corporate Franchise or Income Tax
Submit To: Utah State Tax Commission
Cost: $0
For sales tax exemption:

Form: TC-160: Application for Sales Tax Exemption Number for Religious or Charitable Institutions

Submit To: Utah State Tax Commission
Cost: $0

Step-12: Charitable Solicitation Registration

This is yet another area where it varies between states, but most require it on an annual basis. This means you need to register with the state before fundraising from any resident of the state. Depending on the scope of your organization you may need to register in other states as well.

Overseen By: Utah Department of Commerce - Division of Consumer Protection.

Exemptions:
1. Religious organizations
2. Educational institutions
3. Membership organizations
4. Political groups
5. Appeals for named individuals

To file in Utah, you need to do the following:

Submit To: Utah Department of Commerce - Division of Consumer Protection
How to File: Online
Cost: $78

Step-13: Business Licenses and Permits
From here you will be all set to start your nonprofit. However, the work isn't over yet. You'll also need to stay in compliance with your nonprofit. Next, consider your required annual filings to remain legal.

Annual Renewal

1. IRS Renewals
    a. IRS Form 990
    b. Due the 15th day of the 5th month following the end of the taxable year
2. Utah has no renewal requirements for corporate income tax exemption.
3. Utah has no renewal requirements for sales tax exemption.
4. Utah requires the filing of an annual report
    a. Filed with the Utah Department of Commerce - Division of Corporations
    b. Form Annual Report / Renewal Form
    c. Filed by mail or online
    d. Costs $10
    e. Due annually by the end of the initial registration month
    f. $10 late fee
    g. May be filed by anyone with authority
    h. Doesn't need original signatures
5. Charitable Solicitation Renewal
    a. Filed with the Utah Department of Commerce - Division of Consumer Protection
    b. Filed by online
    c. Costs $78

VERMONT

Step-1: Name Your Nonprofit

The name of your nonprofit will establish its brand and will allow you to incorporate with the state. The name you choose cannot conflict with any other organization registered within the state of Vermont. Make sure the name you choose is available and meets all state requirement. Search through the Vermont Secretary of State - Division of Corporations.

Step-2: Get Initial Directors and Incorporators

The incorporate is the individual who signs the Articles of Incorporation for your business. You will need at least one incorporator, but you can have additional. The directors are the governing body of your nonprofit and are stakeholders in the purpose and success of your nonprofit. You should have at least three directors who are unrelated individuals in order to meet IRS requirements. You'll also want to meet age and residency requirements.

Step-3: Selected a Registered Agent

The registered agent is responsible for receiving legal notices for your nonprofit. A registered agent needs to be physically living in the state and maintain an office open during regular business hours.

Step-4: Articles of Incorporation

The articles of incorporation are the official creation of your nonprofit. They show where and when the nonprofit was formed and provide the necessary information to verify the

nonprofits existence. Make sure your articles of incorporation meet state and IRS requirement.

Form: Articles of Incorporation
Submit To: Vermont Secretary of State - Division of Corporations
How to File: Mail or in person
Cost: $125
Time Frame: About 5-7 days.

Additional Notes:
- File in duplicate with a self-addressed stamped envelope

Step-5: Get an Employer Identification Number (EIN)

This is a unique nine-digit number that the IRS assigned to identify your nonprofit. Your EIN is then used to open a bank account, apply for 501(c)(3) status and submit 990 IRS returns.

Form: IRS Form SS-4
Submit To: Internal Revenue Service (IRS)
How to File: Mail, phone, fax or online
Cost: $0
Time Frame: By phone or online is immediate, by fax is 4 days and by mail is 4-5 weeks.

Additional Notes:
- Print EIN before the closing session

Step-6: Storing Records

As you start a nonprofit, you will be faced with a number of official documents. Be sure you organize and store all of these records together for easy access later.

Step-7: Initial Governing Policies and Documents

The governing document for your nonprofit is your bylaws since they serve as the operating manual for your organization and need to be consistent with both the law and your articles of incorporation. The first meeting of your Board of Directors should be to review and ratify the bylaws.

You should also create and adopt a conflict of interest policy. This will guide you in what to do if someone in a key position within your nonprofit has competing interests and makes a decision that benefits themselves while harming your nonprofit. Organizational interests should be prioritized ahead of personal interests. All conflicts should be disclosed immediately.

Both the bylaws and the conflict of interest policy will need to be approved and adopted before applying to the IRS for 501(c)(3) status.

Step-8: Board of Directors Organizational Meeting

This initial meeting is the most productive and important one. You will approve bylaws, adopt the conflict of interest policy, elect directors, appoint officers and approve any resolutions like opening a bank account. Be sure to record the decisions made in meeting minutes.

Step-9: State Tax Identification Numbers and Accounts

Incorporating a nonprofit means, you will follow all state laws. Requirements vary by state so check with your individual state first.

To file in Vermont:

Form: S-1: Vermont Application for Business Tax Account
Submit To: Vermont Department of Taxes
How to File: Mail or fax
Cost: $0

Step-10: File for 501(c) Status

This can seem like one of the most difficult steps in starting your nonprofit, but it also offers many benefits. After applying and submitting your documents, the IRS will give you a Determination Letter that officially recognizes your tax-exempt status.

Form: IRS Form 1023, Form 1023-EZ or Form 1024
Submit To: Internal Revenue Service (IRS)
How to File: Mail
Cost: $275 for Form 1023-EZ and $600 for Form 1023
Time Frame: Less than a month for Form 1023-EZ and 3-6 months for Form 1023

Step-11: State Tax Exemption

Once you have your IRS Determination Letter, you next need to figure out your state's requirements for tax-exempt status. This is another area that varies by state. You may also need to do periodic renewals for tax-exempt status.

Vermont doesn't have you file for income tax exemption.

Vermont doesn't have you file for sales tax exemption.

Step-12: Charitable Solicitation Registration

This is yet another area where it varies between states, but most require it on an annual basis. This means you need to register with the state before fundraising from any resident of the state. Depending on the scope of your organization you may need to register in other states as well.

Vermont doesn't require this registration.

Step-13: Business Licenses and Permits

From here you will be all set to start your nonprofit. However, the work isn't over yet. You'll also need to stay in compliance with your nonprofit. Next, consider your required annual filings to remain legal.

Annual Renewal

1. IRS Renewals
    a. IRS Form 990
    b. Due the 15th day of the 5th month following the end of the taxable year
2. Vermont has no renewal requirements for corporate income tax exemption.
3. Vermont has no renewal requirements for sales tax exemption.
4. Vermont requires the filing of a biennial report
    a. Filed with the Vermont Secretary of State - Division of Corporations
    b. Filed by mail or online
    c. Costs $20
    d. Due biennially by April 1st.
    e. $25 late fee
    f. May be filed by anyone with authority
    g. Doesn't need original signatures

VIRGINIA

Step-1: Name Your Nonprofit

The name of your nonprofit will establish its brand and will allow you to incorporate with the state. The name you choose cannot conflict with any other organization registered within the state of Virginia. Make sure the name you choose is available and meets all state requirement. Search through the Virginia State Corporation Commission.

Step-2: Get Initial Directors and Incorporators

The incorporate is the individual who signs the Articles of Incorporation for your business. You will need at least one incorporator, but you can have additional. The directors are the governing body of your nonprofit and are stakeholders in the purpose and success of your nonprofit. You should have at least three directors who are unrelated individuals in order to meet IRS requirements. You'll also want to meet age and residency requirements.

Step-3: Selected a Registered Agent

The registered agent is responsible for receiving legal notices for your nonprofit. A registered agent needs to be physically living in the state and maintain an office open during regular business hours.

Step-4: Articles of Incorporation

The articles of incorporation are the official creation of your nonprofit. They show where and when the nonprofit was formed and provide the necessary information to verify the nonprofits existence. Make sure your articles of incorporation meet state and IRS requirement.

Form: Articles of Incorporation of a Virginia Nonstock Corporation
Submit To: Virginia State Corporation Commission
How to File: Mail or online
Cost: $50 charter fee + $25 filing fee = $75 total
Time Frame: About 7 days by mail. About 3-7 days online.

Additional Notes:
- Submit the original signed articles

Step-5: Get an Employer Identification Number (EIN)

This is a unique nine-digit number that the IRS assigned to identify your nonprofit. Your EIN is then used to open a bank account, apply for 501(c)(3) status and submit 990 IRS returns.

Form: IRS Form SS-4
Submit To: Internal Revenue Service (IRS)
How to File: Mail, phone, fax or online
Cost: $0
Time Frame: By phone or online is immediate, by fax is 4 days and by mail is 4-5 weeks.

Additional Notes:
- Print EIN before the closing session

Step-6: Storing Records

As you start a nonprofit, you will be faced with a number of official documents. Be sure you organize and store all of these records together for easy access later.

Step-7: Initial Governing Policies and Documents

The governing document for your nonprofit is your bylaws since they serve as the operating manual for your organization and need to be consistent with both the law and your articles of incorporation. The first meeting of your Board of Directors should be to review and ratify the bylaws.

You should also create and adopt a conflict of interest policy. This will guide you in what to do if someone in a key position within your nonprofit has competing interests and makes a decision that benefits themselves while harming your nonprofit. Organizational interests should be prioritized ahead of personal interests. All conflicts should be disclosed immediately.

Both the bylaws and the conflict of interest policy will need to be approved and adopted before applying to the IRS for 501(c)(3) status.

Step-8: Board of Directors Organizational Meeting

This initial meeting is the most productive and important one. You will approve bylaws, adopt the conflict of interest policy, elect directors, appoint officers and approve any resolutions like opening a bank account. Be sure to record the decisions made in meeting minutes.

Step-9: State Tax Identification Numbers and Accounts

Incorporating a nonprofit means, you will follow all state laws. Requirements vary by state so check with your individual state first.
To file in Virginia:

Form: R-1: Virginia Department of Taxation Business Registration Form
Submit To: Virginia Department of Taxation
How to File: Mail or online

Cost: $0

Step-10: File for 501(c) Status

This can seem like one of the most difficult steps in starting your nonprofit, but it also offers many benefits. After applying and submitting your documents, the IRS will give you a Determination Letter that officially recognizes your tax-exempt status.

Form: IRS Form 1023, Form 1023-EZ or Form 1024
Submit To: Internal Revenue Service (IRS)
How to File: Mail
Cost: $275 for Form 1023-EZ and $600 for Form 1023
Time Frame: Less than a month for Form 1023-EZ and 3-6 months for Form 1023

Step-11: State Tax Exemption

Once you have your IRS Determination Letter, you next need to figure out your state's requirements for tax-exempt status. This is another area that varies by state. You may also need to do periodic renewals for tax-exempt status.

Virginia doesn't have you file for income tax exemption.

To file for sales tax exemption in Virginia:

Form: NP-1: Exemption Application for Nonprofit Organizations
Submit To: Virginia Department of Taxation
Cost: $0

Step-12: Charitable Solicitation Registration

This is yet another area where it varies between states, but most require it on an annual basis. This means you need to register with the state before fundraising from any resident of the state. Depending on the scope of your organization you may need to register in other states as well.

Overseen By: Virginia Office of Charitable and Regulatory Programs.

Exemptions:
1. Less than $5,000 a year and carried out by unpaid volunteers
2. Religious organizations
3. Soliciting grant proposals
4. Political organizations
5. Educational institutions
6. Membership organizations
7. Civic leagues and organizations
8. Appeals for named individuals
9. Non-resident organization

To file, you need to do the following:

Form: URS or OCRP-102: Registration Statement for a Charitable Organization
Submit To: Virginia Office of Charitable and Regulatory Programs
How to File: Mail
Cost: $100 initial registration + $30-325 depending on gross contributions.
Additional Notes:
- File originals - copies not allowed
- Must be signed by president and CFO
- Attach all necessary documents

Step-13: Business Licenses and Permits

From here you will be all set to start your nonprofit. However, the work isn't over yet. You'll also need to stay in compliance with your nonprofit. Next, consider your required annual filings to remain legal.

Annual Renewal

1. IRS Renewals
    a. IRS Form 990
    b. Due the 15th day of the 5th month following the end of the taxable year
2. Virginia Corporate Tax Returns
    a. Filed with Virginia Department of Taxation
    b. Form 500: Corporation Income Tax Return
    c. Due six and a half months after fiscal year end
3. Virginia has no renewal requirements for corporate income tax exemption.
4. To renew sales tax exemption in Virginia
    a. Filed with Virginia Department of Taxation
    b. Form NP-1: Exemption Application for Nonprofit Organizations
    c. Cost $0
    d. Due every 5 years
5. Virginia requires the filing of an annual report
    a. Filed with the Virginia State Corporation Commission
    b. Filed by mail, in person or online
    c. Costs $25
    d. Due annually by the end of the anniversary registration month
    e. $10 late fee
    f. May be filed by an officer or director
    g. Doesn't need original signatures
6. Charitable Solicitation Renewal
    a. Filed with the Virginia Office of Charitable and Regulatory Programs
    b. Form OCRP-102: Registration Statement for a Charitable Organization
    c. Filed by mail

d. Costs $30-250 depending on gross contributions
e. Renewal is annually within four and a half months of the close of the fiscal year
f. File the original - copies aren't allowed
g. Must be signed by the president and CFO
h. Attach an annual financial report

WASHINGTON

Step-1: Name Your Nonprofit

The name of your nonprofit will establish its brand and will allow you to incorporate with the state. The name you choose cannot conflict with any other organization registered within the state of Washington. Make sure the name you choose is available and meets all state requirement. Search through the Washington Secretary of State - Corporations Division.

Step-2: Get Initial Directors and Incorporators

The incorporate is the individual who signs the Articles of Incorporation for your business. You will need at least one incorporator, but you can have additional. The directors are the governing body of your nonprofit and are stakeholders in the purpose and success of your nonprofit. You should have at least three directors who are unrelated individuals in order to meet IRS requirements. You'll also want to meet age and residency requirements.

Step-3: Selected a Registered Agent

The registered agent is responsible for receiving legal notices for your nonprofit. A registered agent needs to be physically living in the state and maintain an office open during regular business hours.

Step-4: Articles of Incorporation

The articles of incorporation are the official creation of your nonprofit. They show where and when the nonprofit was formed and provide the necessary information to verify the

nonprofits existence. Make sure your articles of incorporation meet state and IRS requirement.

Form: Articles of Incorporation - Washington Nonprofit Corporation
Submit To: Washington Secretary of State - Corporations Division
How to File: Mail or online
Cost: $30 by mail. $80 by mail expedite. $50 online.
Time Frame: About 2 months by mail. About 2-3 days by mail expedited or online.

Step-5: Get an Employer Identification Number (EIN)

This is a unique nine-digit number that the IRS assigned to identify your nonprofit. Your EIN is then used to open a bank account, apply for 501(c)(3) status and submit 990 IRS returns.

Form: IRS Form SS-4
Submit To: Internal Revenue Service (IRS)
How to File: Mail, phone, fax or online
Cost: $0
Time Frame: By phone or online is immediate, by fax is 4 days and by mail is 4-5 weeks.

Additional Notes:
- Print EIN before the closing session

Step-6: Storing Records

As you start a nonprofit, you will be faced with a number of official documents. Be sure you organize and store all of these records together for easy access later.

Step-7: Initial Governing Policies and Documents

The governing document for your nonprofit is your bylaws since they serve as the operating manual for your organization and need to be consistent with both the law and your articles of incorporation. The first meeting of your Board of Directors should be to review and ratify the bylaws.

You should also create and adopt a conflict of interest policy. This will guide you in what to do if someone in a key position within your nonprofit has competing interests and makes a decision that benefits themselves while harming your nonprofit. Organizational interests should be prioritized ahead of personal interests. All conflicts should be disclosed immediately.

Both the bylaws and the conflict of interest policy will need to be approved and adopted before applying to the IRS for 501(c)(3) status.

Step-8: Board of Directors Organizational Meeting

This initial meeting is the most productive and important one. You will approve bylaws, adopt the conflict of interest policy, elect directors, appoint officers and approve any resolutions like opening a bank account. Be sure to record the decisions made in meeting minutes.

Step-9: State Tax Identification Numbers and Accounts

Incorporating a nonprofit means, you will follow all state laws. Requirements vary by state so check with your individual state first.

To file in Washington:

Form: BLS-700-028: Washington Business License Application
Submit To: Washington Department of Revenue

How to File: Mail or online
Cost: $19
Time Frame: About 2 days online. About 21 days by mail.

Step-10: File for 501(c) Status

This can seem like one of the most difficult steps in starting your nonprofit, but it also offers many benefits. After applying and submitting your documents, the IRS will give you a Determination Letter that officially recognizes your tax-exempt status.

Form: IRS Form 1023, Form 1023-EZ or Form 1024
Submit To: Internal Revenue Service (IRS)
How to File: Mail
Cost: $275 for Form 1023-EZ and $600 for Form 1023
Time Frame: Less than a month for Form 1023-EZ and 3-6 months for Form 1023

Step-11: State Tax Exemption

Once you have your IRS Determination Letter, you next need to figure out your state's requirements for tax-exempt status. This is another area that varies by state. You may also need to do periodic renewals for tax-exempt status.

For income tax and sales tax exemption in Washington, you need to contact the Washington Department of Revenue.

Step-12: Charitable Solicitation Registration

This is yet another area where it varies between states, but most require it on an annual basis. This means you need to register with the state before fundraising from any

resident of the state. Depending on the scope of your organization you may need to register in other states as well.

Overseen By: Washington Secretary of State - Charities Program

To file in Washington, you need to do the following:

Form: Charitable Organization Registration / Renewal
Submit To: Washington Secretary of State - Charities Program
How to File: Mail
Cost: $60 + $20 online fee. Optional $50 expedite fee for 2-3 day processing.

Additional Notes:
- Attach all necessary documents

Step-13: Business Licenses and Permits

From here you will be all set to start your nonprofit. However, the work isn't over yet. You'll also need to stay in compliance with your nonprofit. Next, consider your required annual filings to remain legal.

Annual Renewal

1. IRS Renewals
    a. IRS Form 990
    b. Due the 15th day of the 5th month following the end of the taxable year
2. Washington Corporate Tax Returns
    a. Filed with Washington Department of Revenue
    b. Form Combined Excise Tax Return
    c. Due January 31st

3. Washington has no renewal requirements for corporate income tax exemption.
4. Washington has no renewal requirements for sales tax exemption.
5. Washington requires the filing of an annual review
    a. Filed with the Washington Secretary of State - Corporations Division
    b. Form Annual Report
    c. Filed by mail or online
    d. Costs $10. $50 expedite fee.
    e. Due annually by the end of the anniversary registration month
    f. $25 late fee
    g. May be filed by anyone with authority
    h. Doesn't need original signatures
6. Charitable Solicitation Renewal
    a. Filed with the Washington Secretary of State - Charities Program
    b. Form Charitable Organization Registration / Renewal
    c. Filed by mail
    d. Costs $40 + $20 online fee. Optional $50 expedite fee for processing in 2-3 days.
    e. Renewal is annually within 11 months of the close of the fiscal year
    f. Attach an annual financial report

WEST VIRGINIA

Step-1: Name Your Nonprofit

The name of your nonprofit will establish its brand and will allow you to incorporate with the state. The name you choose cannot conflict with any other organization registered within the state of West Virginia. Make sure the name you choose is available and meets all state requirement. Search through the West Virginia Secretary of State - Business and Licensing Division.

Step-2: Get Initial Directors and Incorporators

The incorporate is the individual who signs the Articles of Incorporation for your business. You will need at least one incorporator, but you can have additional. The directors are the governing body of your nonprofit and are stakeholders in the purpose and success of your nonprofit. You should have at least three directors who are unrelated individuals in order to meet IRS requirements. You'll also want to meet age and residency requirements.

Step-3: Selected a Registered Agent

The registered agent is responsible for receiving legal notices for your nonprofit. A registered agent needs to be physically living in the state and maintain an office open during regular business hours.

Step-4: Articles of Incorporation

The articles of incorporation are the official creation of your nonprofit. They show where and when the nonprofit was formed and provide the necessary information to verify the

nonprofits existence. Make sure your articles of incorporation meet state and IRS requirement.

Form: CD-1NP: Articles of Incorporation with Nonprofit IRS Attachment
Submit To: West Virginia Secretary of State - Business and Licensing Division
How to File: Mail or online
Cost: $25
Time Frame: About 1-2 business days

Additional Notes:
- Submit the original and one copy

Step-5: Get an Employer Identification Number (EIN)

This is a unique nine-digit number that the IRS assigned to identify your nonprofit. Your EIN is then used to open a bank account, apply for 501(c)(3) status and submit 990 IRS returns.

Form: IRS Form SS-4
Submit To: Internal Revenue Service (IRS)
How to File: Mail, phone, fax or online
Cost: $0
Time Frame: By phone or online is immediate, by fax is 4 days and by mail is 4-5 weeks.

Additional Notes:
- Print EIN before the closing session

Step-6: Storing Records

As you start a nonprofit, you will be faced with a number of official documents. Be sure you organize and store all of these records together for easy access later.

Step-7: Initial Governing Policies and Documents

The governing document for your nonprofit is your bylaws since they serve as the operating manual for your organization and need to be consistent with both the law and your articles of incorporation. The first meeting of your Board of Directors should be to review and ratify the bylaws.

You should also create and adopt a conflict of interest policy. This will guide you in what to do if someone in a key position within your nonprofit has competing interests and makes a decision that benefits themselves while harming your nonprofit. Organizational interests should be prioritized ahead of personal interests. All conflicts should be disclosed immediately.

Both the bylaws and the conflict of interest policy will need to be approved and adopted before applying to the IRS for 501(c)(3) status.

Step-8: Board of Directors Organizational Meeting

This initial meeting is the most productive and important one. You will approve bylaws, adopt the conflict of interest policy, elect directors, appoint officers and approve any resolutions like opening a bank account. Be sure to record the decisions made in meeting minutes.

Step-9: State Tax Identification Numbers and Accounts

Incorporating a nonprofit means, you will follow all state laws. Requirements vary by state so check with your individual state first.

To file in West Virginia:

Form: WV/BUS-APP: West Virginia Office of Business Registration
Submit To: West Virginia State Tax Department
How to File: Mail or online
Cost: $0

Step-10: File for 501(c) Status

This can seem like one of the most difficult steps in starting your nonprofit, but it also offers many benefits. After applying and submitting your documents, the IRS will give you a Determination Letter that officially recognizes your tax-exempt status.

Form: IRS Form 1023, Form 1023-EZ or Form 1024
Submit To: Internal Revenue Service (IRS)
How to File: Mail
Cost: $275 for Form 1023-EZ and $600 for Form 1023
Time Frame: Less than a month for Form 1023-EZ and 3-6 months for Form 1023

Step-11: State Tax Exemption

Once you have your IRS Determination Letter, you next need to figure out your state's requirements for tax-exempt status. This is another area that varies by state. You may also need to do periodic renewals for tax-exempt status.

For income tax exemption in West Virginia contact the West Virginia State Tax Department.

For sales tax exemption in West Virginia:
Form: F0003: Streamlined Sales and Use Tax Certificate of Exemption

Submit To: West Virginia State Tax Department
Cost: $0

Step-12: Charitable Solicitation Registration

This is yet another area where it varies between states, but most require it on an annual basis. This means you need to register with the state before fundraising from any resident of the state. Depending on the scope of your organization you may need to register in other states as well.

Overseen By: West Virginia Secretary of State - Charitable Organizations Division.

Exemptions:
1. Less than $25,000 per the calendar year from the public and grants
2. Religious organizations
3. Educational institutions
4. Hospitals
5. Membership organizations
6. Appeals for individuals

To file in Washington, you need to do the following:

Form: Registration of Charitable Organization
Submit To: West Virginia Secretary of State - Charitable Organizations Division
How to File: Mail
Cost: $15-50 depending on the type of nonprofit organization.

Additional Notes:
- Attach all necessary documents
- Must be signed by the CFO and another authorized officer

- Signatures need to be notarized

Step-13: Business Licenses and Permits

From here you will be all set to start your nonprofit. However, the work isn't over yet. You'll also need to stay in compliance with your nonprofit. Next, consider your required annual filings to remain legal.

Annual Renewal

1. IRS Renewals
    a. IRS Form 990
    b. Due the 15th day of the 5th month following the end of the taxable year
2. West Virginia Corporate Tax Returns
    a. Filed with West Virginia State Tax Department
    b. Form Corporate Net Income / Business Franchise Tax Return
    c. Due four and half months after the close of the fiscal year
3. West Virginia has no renewal requirements for corporate income tax exemption.
4. West Virginia has no renewal requirements for sales tax exemption.
5. West Virginia requires the filing of an annual report
    a. Filed with the West Virginia Secretary of State - Business and Licensing Division
    b. Filed by mail or online
    c. Costs $25
    d. Due annually by July 1st
    e. $25 late fee
    f. May be filed by anyone with authority
    g. Doesn't need original signatures
6. Charitable Solicitation Renewal

a. Filed with the West Virginia Secretary of State - Charitable Organizations Division
b. Form Registration of Charitable Organization
c. Filed by mail
d. Costs $15-50 depending on the type of nonprofit organization
e. Renewal is annually by the anniversary of the registration date
f. Attach an annual financial report
g. Needs to be signed by the CFO and an authorized officer
h. Signatures need to be notarized

WISCONSIN

Step-1: Name Your Nonprofit

The name of your nonprofit will establish its brand and will allow you to incorporate with the state. The name you choose cannot conflict with any other organization registered within the state of Wisconsin. Make sure the name you choose is available and meets all state requirement. Search through the Wisconsin Department of Financial Institutions - Corporation Section.

Step-2: Get Initial Directors and Incorporators

The incorporate is the individual who signs the Articles of Incorporation for your business. You will need at least one incorporator, but you can have additional. The directors are the governing body of your nonprofit and are stakeholders in the purpose and success of your nonprofit. You should have at least three directors who are unrelated individuals in order to meet IRS requirements. You'll also want to meet age and residency requirements.

Step-3: Selected a Registered Agent

The registered agent is responsible for receiving legal notices for your nonprofit. A registered agent needs to be physically living in the state and maintain an office open during regular business hours.

Step-4: Articles of Incorporation

The articles of incorporation are the official creation of your nonprofit. They show where and when the nonprofit was formed and provide the necessary information to verify the

nonprofits existence. Make sure your articles of incorporation meet state and IRS requirement.

Form: Articles of Incorporation
Submit To: Wisconsin Department of Financial Institutions - Corporation Section
How to File: Mail
Cost: $35
Time Frame: About 4-7 days

Additional Notes:
- Submit the original and one copy

Step-5: Get an Employer Identification Number (EIN)

This is a unique nine-digit number that the IRS assigned to identify your nonprofit. Your EIN is then used to open a bank account, apply for 501(c)(3) status and submit 990 IRS returns.

Form: IRS Form SS-4
Submit To: Internal Revenue Service (IRS)
How to File: Mail, phone, fax or online
Cost: $0
Time Frame: By phone or online is immediate, by fax is 4 days and by mail is 4-5 weeks.

Additional Notes:
- Print EIN before the closing session

Step-6: Storing Records

As you start a nonprofit, you will be faced with a number of official documents. Be sure you organize and store all of these records together for easy access later.

Step-7: Initial Governing Policies and Documents

The governing document for your nonprofit is your bylaws since they serve as the operating manual for your organization and need to be consistent with both the law and your articles of incorporation. The first meeting of your Board of Directors should be to review and ratify the bylaws.

You should also create and adopt a conflict of interest policy. This will guide you in what to do if someone in a key position within your nonprofit has competing interests and makes a decision that benefits themselves while harming your nonprofit. Organizational interests should be prioritized ahead of personal interests. All conflicts should be disclosed immediately.

Both the bylaws and the conflict of interest policy will need to be approved and adopted before applying to the IRS for 501(c)(3) status.

Step-8: Board of Directors Organizational Meeting

This initial meeting is the most productive and important one. You will approve bylaws, adopt the conflict of interest policy, elect directors, appoint officers and approve any resolutions like opening a bank account. Be sure to record the decisions made in meeting minutes.

Step-9: State Tax Identification Numbers and Accounts

Incorporating a nonprofit means, you will follow all state laws. Requirements vary by state so check with your individual state first.

To file in Wisconsin:

Form: BTR-101: Application for Business Tax Registration
Submit To: Wisconsin Department of Revenue
How to File: Mail, fax or online
Cost: $20
Time Frame: About 15 days

Step-10: File for 501(c) Status

This can seem like one of the most difficult steps in starting your nonprofit, but it also offers many benefits. After applying and submitting your documents, the IRS will give you a Determination Letter that officially recognizes your tax-exempt status.

Form: IRS Form 1023, Form 1023-EZ or Form 1024
Submit To: Internal Revenue Service (IRS)
How to File: Mail
Cost: $275 for Form 1023-EZ and $600 for Form 1023
Time Frame: Less than a month for Form 1023-EZ and 3-6 months for Form 1023

Step-11: State Tax Exemption

Once you have your IRS Determination Letter, you next need to figure out your state's requirements for tax-exempt status. This is another area that varies by state. You may also need to do periodic renewals for tax-exempt status.

Wisconsin doesn't require you to file for income tax exemption.

For sales tax exemption in Wisconsin:
Form: S-103: Application for Wisconsin Sales and Use Tax Certificate of Exempt Status

Submit To: Wisconsin Department of Revenue
Cost: $0

Step-12: Charitable Solicitation Registration

This is yet another area where it varies between states, but most require it on an annual basis. This means you need to register with the state before fundraising from any resident of the state. Depending on the scope of your organization you may need to register in other states as well.

Overseen By: Wisconsin Department of Financial Institutions - Division of Banking.

Exemptions:
1. Less than $5,000 per fiscal year
2. Religious organizations
3. Educational institutions
4. Political groups or individuals
5. Membership organizations
6. Appeals for individuals
7. Veterans organizations

To file in Wisconsin you need to do the following:

Form: 296: Charitable Organization Registration Application
Submit To: Wisconsin Department of Financial Institutions - Division of Banking
How to File: Mail
Cost: $15
Additional Notes:
- Attach all necessary documents
- Must be signed by the CFO and president

- Signatures need to be notarized

Step-13: Business Licenses and Permits

From here you will be all set to start your nonprofit. However, the work isn't over yet. You'll also need to stay in compliance with your nonprofit. Next, consider your required annual filings to remain legal.

Annual Renewal

1. IRS Renewals
    a. IRS Form 990
    b. Due the 15th day of the 5th month following the end of the taxable year
2. Wisconsin has no renewal requirements for corporate income tax exemption.
3. Wisconsin has no renewal requirements for sales tax exemption.
4. Wisconsin requires the filing of an annual report
    a. Filed with the Wisconsin Department of Financial Institutions - Corporation Section
    b. Filed by mail or online
    c. Costs $10
    d. Takes about 5 days to process
    e. Due annually by the end of anniversary registration
    f. May be filed by anyone with authority
    g. Doesn't need original signatures
5. Charitable Solicitation Renewal
    a. Filed with the Wisconsin Department of Financial Institutions - Division of Banking
    b. Filed online
    c. Costs $54
    d. Renewal is annually by July 31st

e. $25 late fee

WYOMING

Step-1: Name Your Nonprofit

The name of your nonprofit will establish its brand and will allow you to incorporate with the state. The name you choose cannot conflict with any other organization registered within the state of Wyoming. Make sure the name you choose is available and meets all state requirement. Search through the Wyoming Secretary of State - Business Division.

Step-2: Get Initial Directors and Incorporators

The incorporate is the individual who signs the Articles of Incorporation for your business. You will need at least one incorporator, but you can have additional. The directors are the governing body of your nonprofit and are stakeholders in the purpose and success of your nonprofit. You should have at least three directors who are unrelated individuals in order to meet IRS requirements. You'll also want to meet age and residency requirements.

Step-3: Selected a Registered Agent

The registered agent is responsible for receiving legal notices for your nonprofit. A registered agent needs to be physically living in the state and maintain an office open during regular business hours.

Step-4: Articles of Incorporation

The articles of incorporation are the official creation of your nonprofit. They show where and when the nonprofit was formed and provide the necessary information to verify the nonprofits existence. Make sure your articles of incorporation meet state and IRS requirement.

Form: Incorporation Articles

Submit To: Wyoming Secretary of State - Business Division

How to File: Mail

Cost: $25

Time Frame: About 3-5 days

Additional Notes:

- Submit the original signed document

Step-5: Get an Employer Identification Number (EIN)

This is a unique nine-digit number that the IRS assigned to identify your nonprofit. Your EIN is then used to open a bank account, apply for 501(c)(3) status and submit 990 IRS returns.

Form: IRS Form SS-4

Submit To: Internal Revenue Service (IRS)

How to File: Mail, phone, fax or online

Cost: $0

Time Frame: By phone or online is immediate, by fax is 4 days and by mail is 4-5 weeks.

Additional Notes:

- Print EIN before the closing session

Step-6: Storing Records

As you start a nonprofit, you will be faced with a number of official documents. Be sure you organize and store all of these records together for easy access later.

Step-7: Initial Governing Policies and Documents

The governing document for your nonprofit is your bylaws since they serve as the operating manual for your organization and need to be consistent with both the law and your articles of incorporation. The first meeting of your Board of Directors should be to review and ratify the bylaws.

You should also create and adopt a conflict of interest policy. This will guide you in what to do if someone in a key position within your nonprofit has competing interests and makes a decision that benefits themselves while harming your nonprofit. Organizational interests should be prioritized ahead of personal interests. All conflicts should be disclosed immediately.

Both the bylaws and the conflict of interest policy will need to be approved and adopted before applying to the IRS for 501(c)(3) status.

Step-8: Board of Directors Organizational Meeting

This initial meeting is the most productive and important one. You will approve bylaws, adopt the conflict of interest policy, elect directors, appoint officers and approve any resolutions like opening a bank account. Be sure to record the decisions made in meeting minutes.

Step-9: Update Registered Agent Records

Within 60 days of filing Articles of Incorporation you need to provide information of a registered agent including the following:
1. Names and addresses of each entity's directors, officers, managers, partners, trustees or persons serving in any capacity.
2. The name, address and business phone number of a natural person who serves as an officer, director, employee or designated agent of each entity represented who is authorized to receive communications.

3. A copy of the written contract or agreement creating a relationship between an agency and the registered agent with respect to accepting service of process.

Step-10: State Tax Identification Numbers and Accounts

Incorporating a nonprofit means, you will follow all state laws. Requirements vary by state so check with your individual state first.

Wyoming doesn't apply a corporate income tax or a sales/use tax.

Step-11: File for 501(c) Status

This can seem like one of the most difficult steps in starting your nonprofit, but it also offers many benefits. After applying and submitting your documents, the IRS will give you a Determination Letter that officially recognizes your tax-exempt status.

Form: IRS Form 1023, Form 1023-EZ or Form 1024
Submit To: Internal Revenue Service (IRS)
How to File: Mail
Cost: $275 for Form 1023-EZ and $600 for Form 1023
Time Frame: Less than a month for Form 1023-EZ and 3-6 months for Form 1023

Step-12: State Tax Exemption
Once you have your IRS Determination Letter, you next need to figure out your state's requirements for tax-exempt status. This is another area that varies by state. You may also need to do periodic renewals for tax-exempt status.

Wyoming doesn't require you to file for income tax exemption.

For sales tax exemption in Wyoming contact the Wyoming Department of Revenue.

Step-13: Charitable Solicitation Registration

This is yet another area where it varies between states, but most require it on an annual basis. This means you need to register with the state before fundraising from any resident of the state. Depending on the scope of your organization you may need to register in other states as well.

This registration is not required in Wyoming.

Step-14: Business Licenses and Permits

From here you will be all set to start your nonprofit. However, the work isn't over yet. You'll also need to stay in compliance with your nonprofit. Next, consider your required annual filings to remain legal.

Annual Renewal

1. IRS Renewals
    a. IRS Form 990
    b. Due the 15th day of the 5th month following the end of the taxable year
2. Wyoming has no renewal requirements for corporate income tax exemption.
3. Wyoming has no renewal requirements for sales tax exemption.
4. Wyoming requires the filing of an annual report
    a. Filed with the Wyoming Secretary of State - Business Division
    b. Filed by mail or online
    c. Costs $25 + $2-$9 convenience fee for filing online
    d. Due annually by the first day of anniversary registration month
    e. May be filed by anyone with authority
    f. Requires original signatures

APPENDIX – 1

SAMPLE ARTICLES OF INCORPORATION

NONPROFIT CORPORATION ARTICLES OF INCORPORATION

Pursuant to §_____ of the laws of [Keywords], the undersigned majority of whom are citizens of the United States, do hereby submit these Articles of Incorporation for the purpose of forming a nonprofit corporation.

ARTICLE 1
Name

The name of the corporation is: [Comments]

ARTICLE 2
Existence

The corporation shall have perpetual existence.

ARTICLE 3
Effective Date

The effective date of incorporation shall be: <u>upon filing by the Secretary of State</u>.

ARTICLE 4
Members

The corporation <u>will or will not</u> have members

ARTICLE 5
Type of nonprofit corporation

The corporation is not for profit and a <u>Public Benefit Corporation, a Mutual Benefit Corporation, or a Religious Corporation</u>

ARTICLE 6

Registered Agent and Office

The street address of the initial registered office of the corporation is:
Address 1
Address 2
The name of the initial registered agent is:

Name of agent Inc.

ARTICLE 7
Principal Office

The corporation has a principal office. The street address of the principal office is:
Address 1
Address 2
County

ARTICLE 8
Mailing Address
Address 1
Address 2
County

ARTICLE 9
Directors

The corporation's initial directors are as follows:

Name, Address 1, Address 2
Name, Address 1, Address 2
Name, Address 1, Address 2

ARTICLE 10
Indemnification

The corporation does indemnify any directors, officers, employees, incorporators, and members of the corporation from any liability regarding the corporation and the affairs of the corporation, unless the person fraudulently and intentionally violated the law and/or maliciously conducted acts to damage and/or defraud the corporation, or as otherwise provided under applicable statute.

ARTICLE 11
Purpose

The purpose of the corporation is exclusively for charitable, religious, educational, and scientific purposes, including, for such purposes, the making of distributions to organizations that qualify as exempt organizations under section 501(c)(3) of the internal revenue code, or the corresponding section of any future federal tax code and herein stated as follows:

<u>Explain why is the corporation being formed, what does it intend to accomplish, who will benefit from its accomplishments, and how will the corporation achieve its purpose.</u>

The character and essence of the corporation is the same as the purpose.

ARTICLE 12
Prohibited Activities

No part of the net earnings of the corporation shall inure to the benefit of, or be distributable to its members, trustees, officers, or other private persons, except that the corporation shall be authorized and empowered to pay reasonable compensation for services rendered and to make payments and distributions in furtherance of the purposes set forth in Article 11. No substantial part of the activities of the corporation shall be the carrying on of propaganda, or otherwise attempting to influence legislation, and the corporation shall not participate in, or intervene in (including the publishing or distribution of statements) any political campaign on behalf of or in opposition to any candidate for public office. Notwithstanding any other provision of these articles, this corporation shall not, except to an insubstantial degree, engage in any activities or exercise any powers that are not in furtherance of the purposes of this corporation.

ARTICLE 13
Distributions Upon Dissolution

Upon the dissolution of the corporation, after paying or making provisions for the payment of all the legal liabilities of the corporation, assets shall be distributed for one or more exempt purposes within the meaning of section 501(c)(3) of the Internal Revenue Code, or the corresponding section of any future federal tax code, or shall be distributed to the federal government, or to a state or local government, for a public purpose. Any such assets not so disposed of shall be disposed of by a court of competent jurisdiction of the county in which the principal office of the corporation is then located, exclusively for such purposes or to such organization or organizations, as said court shall determine which are organized and operated exclusively for such purposes.

ARTICLE 14
Incorporator

The name and address of the Incorporator is:

<u>Name</u>
<u>Address 1</u>
<u>Address 2</u>

_____
Signature

Credit: Courtesy of
https://www.northwestregisteredagent.com

APPENDIX – 2

SAMPLE CONFLICT OF INTEREST POLICES

SAMPLE CONFLICT OF INTEREST POLICIES

NOTE ON THE SCOPE OF THIS MATERIAL

This material is designed to provide general guidance about an aspect of nonprofit corporate governance in the specific and limited context of the governance questions contained in the new IRS Form 990 (published by the IRS in 2008 and applicable to 990 filers based on a 2009-2011 filing year phase-in period depending on the size of the nonprofit). It is intended to provide some general guidance on the establishment of processes and/or policies to address a specific governance question in the Form. The subject matter of that question implicates a broad array of legal and practical issues ranging far beyond the immediate subject matter of the question itself. This material may address some of those issues but does NOT attempt to review them comprehensively and is NOT intended to be relied on for guidance on how they should be addressed in any specific situation.

Whether or not a nonprofit organization adopts a specific governance process or policy (or modifies an existing one), either in response to the disclosure requirements of the new IRS Form 990 or to change its governance practices for other reasons is a matter to be carefully considered by that organization, with input from its board and advisors and evaluation of its specific circumstances. The IRS has explicitly stated that adoption of the policies and practices about which the new Form 990 asks is not mandatory, although the IRS has also indicated that it attaches significance to the manner in which all tax-exempt nonprofit organizations govern themselves. This sample policy is not intended to suggest that the policy is appropriate for every nonprofit organization nor that, if a policy on that topic is determined to be appropriate, the formulation in the sample necessarily fits the needs of an individual nonprofit organization. A customized approach, with outside professional advice, is recommended. Accordingly, this material is intended as general information for legal practitioners advising nonprofit organizations as to their governance and does not constitute legal advice for any particular nonprofit organization. For more information, see the related Form 990 Policy Series Memorandum at: http://www.publiccounsel.org/tools/assets/files/CoIMemo.pdf.

Although the subject matter of this material may have relevance to nonprofit organizations that are not required to file informational tax returns with the IRS or are permitted to file on an IRS form other than Form 990, the focus of this material is 990 filers. While this material is meant to apply to Form 990 filers who are exempt under Section 501(c) of the Internal Revenue Code, certain portions of this material may be applicable only to Section 501(c)(3) organizations. In addition, although this material may be of assistance with respect to nonprofit organizations that are not subject to oversight under California law, there may be portions of this material that are relevant only to nonprofits organized under, or (by reason of their California-related activities) otherwise subject to, California law.

The reader has permission to copy, modify and otherwise use this policy for the reader's or his or her client's use. All other rights are reserved by the copyright holder.

Sample Policy A: California Public Benefit or Religious Corporations; Narrow Range of Covered Persons; Broad Range of Covered Interests; Annual Disclosure of Potential Conflicts of Interest. The following policy includes a conflict of interest policy intended for a California nonprofit public benefit or religious corporation exempt from federal income tax under Code Section 501(c)(3), an annual acknowledgment form, and an annual disclosure of interests that could give rise to a conflict of interest. The policy reflects the following choices:

1. <u>Narrow Range of Covered Persons</u>. The policy is **narrow** in terms of covered persons; it applies to officers, directors, and key employees ONLY. It does not cover all insiders that are disqualified persons under Code Section 4958, and it does cover key employees using the definition from the Form 990 Instructions (which is not part of Code Section 4958). This range of coverage may be appropriate for an organization that wishes to have in place a conflict of policy that meets the minimum requirements necessary to answer "Yes" to Lines 12a-c of Part VI.B, or an organization that wishes to have a separate conflict of interest policy that meets allows it to answer "Yes" to these questions, and separate policies that set forth the policy and procedure for dealing with the conflicts of interests of other persons.

2. <u>Broad Range of Covered Interests</u>. The policy is broad in scope; it applies broadly to all interests potentially affecting a person's judgment, not just financial and not just those regulated by federal tax law or state corporate law. Some organizations will prefer a narrower scope, focusing only on interests and transactions that are regulated by law.

3. <u>Covered Transactions and Relationships</u>. While the policy is designed to pick up many transactions and relationships to be disclosed on Form 990, it may not reach all of them. An organization may need a more detailed disclosure form to collect all the information requested on other parts of current or future versions of Form 990.

4. <u>Disclosure of Family Relationships</u>. The form limits disclosure of family members to those presenting a specific potential conflict. Please be aware that the IRS *may* want names of all listed relatives. Be aware that, pending clarification by the IRS,

not listing all relatives may not be sufficient disclosure to answer "Yes" to Part VI.B, Line12c.

5. <u>Prior Transactions Not Addressed</u>. This policy does not address the approval process for past transactions that have already occurred or commenced.

6. <u>Statutory Compliance Not Guaranteed</u>. Compliance with this sample policy ***does not guarantee compliance*** with Code Section 4958 or other applicable rules of law, including California state corporate law.

7. <u>The Board of Directors as Arbiter of Conflicts</u>. This sample policy assumes that the Board of Directors will be the arbiter of conflicts, and not a committee of the Board or, in the case of religious corporations, the members.

[NAME OF ORGANIZATION]

CONFLICT OF INTEREST POLICY[1]

Article I: Purpose

This conflict of interest policy is designed to foster public confidence in the integrity of [Name of Organization] (the "Organization") and to protect the Organization's interest when it is contemplating entering a transaction (defined below) that might benefit the private interest of a director, a corporate officer, the top management or top financial official, or a key employee (defined below). [Note to Organization: Compliance with this Sample Policy A will not insure compliance with Code Section 4958 or CCC Section 5233 or 9243. Although the range of interests covered by this policy may be broader than those covered by law, the range of covered persons is narrower. Additional procedures may apply to transactions covered by Code Section 4958 or CCC Section 5233 or 9243.]

Article II: Definitions

The following are considered *insiders* for the purposes of this policy:

1. Each member of the Board of Directors or other governing body.

2. The president, chief executive officer, chief operating officer, treasurer and chief financial officer, executive director, or any person with the responsibilities of any of these positions (whether or not the person is an officer of the Organization under the Organization's Bylaws and the

---

[1] Note that this Conflict of Interest Policy does not assume the existence of a separate Compensation Policy. Compensation paid to insiders, including for their service as directors, officers, and key employees, should be evaluated under this Policy in its current form. If an organization has a separate Compensation Policy that addresses such compensation decisions, this sample policy may be modified accordingly.

California Corporations Code).

3. Any *key employee*, meaning an employee whose total annual compensation (including benefits) from the organization and its affiliates is more than $150,000 **and** who (a) has responsibilities or influence over the organization similar to that of officers, directors, or trustees; **or** (b) manages a program that represents 10% or more of the activities, assets, income, or expenses of the organization; **or** (c) has or shares authority to control 10% or more of the organization's capital expenditures, operating budget, or compensation for employees.

Interest means any commitment, investment, relationship, obligation, or involvement, financial or otherwise, direct or indirect, that may influence a person's judgment, including receipt of compensation from the Organization, a sale, loan, or exchange transaction with the Organization.

A *conflict of interest* is present when, in the judgment of the Board of Directors, an insider's stake in the transaction is such that it reduces the likelihood that an insider's influence can be exercised impartially in the best interests of the Organization.

Transaction means any transaction, agreement, or arrangement between an insider and the Organization, or between the Organization and any third party where an insider has an interest in the transaction or any party to it. **[Note to Organization: If the Organization has a separate Compensation Policy that addresses the receipt of compensation by an insider in his or her capacity as an insider (e.g., compensation paid to the President for her services to the Organization as its President), please include the following sentence:** "*Transaction* **does not include compensation arrangements between the Organization and a director, officer, or other insider that are wholly addressed under the Organization's Compensation Policy."]**

Article III: Procedures

1. Duty to Disclose

Each insider shall disclose to the Board all material facts regarding his or her interest in the transaction, promptly upon learning of the proposed transaction.

2. Determining Whether a Conflict of Interest Exists

With regard to an insider, the Board shall determine if a conflict of interest exists. The insider(s) and any other interested person(s) involved with the transaction shall not be present during the Board's discussion or determination of whether a conflict of interest exists, except as provided in Article IV below.

3. Procedures for Addressing a Conflict of Interest

The Board shall follow the procedures set forth in Article IV in order to decide what measures are needed to protect the Organization's interests in light of the nature and seriousness of the conflict, to decide whether to enter into the transaction and, if so, to ensure that the terms of the transaction are appropriate.

Article IV: Review by the Board

The Board may ask questions of and receive presentation(s) from the insider(s) and any other interested person(s), but shall deliberate and vote on the transaction in their absence. The Board shall ascertain that all material facts regarding the transaction and the insider's conflict of interest have been disclosed to the Board and shall compile appropriate data, such as comparability studies, to determine fair market value for the transaction.

After exercising due diligence, which may include investigating alternatives that present no conflict, the Board shall determine whether the transaction is in the Organization's best interest, for its own benefit, and whether it is fair and reasonable to the Organization; the majority of disinterested members of the Board then in office may approve the transaction.

Article V: Records of Proceedings

The minutes of any meeting of the Board pursuant to this policy shall contain the name of each insider who disclosed or was otherwise determined to have an interest in a transaction; the nature of the interest and whether it was determined to constitute a conflict of interest; any alternative transactions considered; the members of the Board who were present during the deliberations on the transaction, those who voted on it, and to what extent interested persons were excluded from the deliberations; any comparability data or other information obtained and relied upon by the Board and how the information was obtained; and the result of the vote, including, if applicable, the terms of the transaction that was approved and the date it was approved.

Article VI: Annual Disclosure and Compliance Statements

Each director, each corporate officer, the top management official, the top financial official, and each key employee of the Organization, shall annually sign a statement on the form attached, that:

- affirms that the person has received a copy of this conflict of interest policy, has read and understood the policy, and has agreed to comply with the policy; and

- discloses the person's financial interests and family relationships that could give rise to conflicts of interest.

Article VII: Violations

If the Board has reasonable cause to believe that an insider of the Organization has failed to disclose actual or possible conflicts of interest, including those arising from a transaction with a related interested person, it shall inform such insider of the basis for this belief and afford the insider an opportunity to explain the alleged failure to disclose. If, after hearing the insider's response and making further investigation as warranted by the circumstances, the Board determines that the insider has failed to disclose an actual or possible conflict of interest, the Board shall take appropriate disciplinary and corrective action.

Article VIII: Annual Reviews

To ensure that the Organization operates in a manner consistent with its status as an organization exempt from federal income tax, the Board shall authorize and oversee an annual review of the administration of this conflict of interest policy. The review may be written or oral. The review shall consider the level of compliance with the policy, the continuing suitability of the policy, and whether the policy should be modified and improved.

[NAME OF ORGANIZATION]

ACKNOWLEDGMENT AND FINANCIAL INTEREST DISCLOSURE STATEMENT

[Name of Organization] (The "Organization") follows a conflict of interest policy designed to foster public confidence in our integrity and to protect our interest when we are contemplating entering a transaction or arrangement that might benefit the private interest of a director, a corporate officer, our top management official and top financial official, or any of our key employees.

Part I. **Acknowledgment of Receipt**

I hereby acknowledge that I have received a copy of the conflict of interest policy of [Name], have read and understood it, and agree to comply with its terms.

_____   _____
Signature   Date

Part II.   Disclosure of Financial Interests

We are required annually to file Form 990 with the Internal Revenue Service, and the form we file is available to the public. To complete Form 990 fully and accurately, we need each officer, director and key employee to disclose the information requested in this Part II.

Part II   Please check ONE of the following boxes:

☐   My interests and relationships have not changed since my last disclosure of interests. [Proceed to signature block below. Do not complete the tables.]

OR

☐   I hereby disclose or update my interests and relationships that could give rise to a conflict of interest: [Complete the table below. Use additional pages as needed.]

Family Relationships	Names of those presenting a potential conflict of interest
Include spouse/domestic partner, living ancestors, brothers and sisters (whether whole or half-blood), children (whether natural or adopted), grandchildren, great grand-children, and spouses/ domestic partners of brothers, sisters, children, grandchildren, and great grandchildren	

Type of interest	Description of interest that could lead to a conflict of interest
Transactions or arrangements with the Organization	
Transactions or affiliations with other nonprofit organizations	
Substantial business or investment holdings	
Transactions or affiliations with businesses not listed above	

I am not aware of any financial interest involving me or a family member that could present a conflict of interest that I have not disclosed either above or in a previous disclosure statement.

_____   _____

A "conflict of interest," for purposes of Form 990, arises when a person in a position of authority over an organization, such as an officer, director, or key employee, may benefit financially from a decision he or she could make in such capacity, including indirect benefits such as to family members or businesses with which the person is closely associated.

B. *Sample Policy B: California Mutual Benefit Corporations; Narrow Range of Covered Persons; Narrow Range of Covered Interests; Annual Disclosure of Potential Conflicts of Interest.* The following policy includes a conflict of interest policy intended for a California nonprofit mutual benefit corporation exempt under Code Section 501(c)(5), (6), or (7), an annual acknowledgment form, and an annual disclosure of interests that could give rise to a conflict of interest. The policy reflects the following choices:

1. <u>Narrow Range of Covered Persons</u>. Like Sample Policy A, Sample Policy B is **narrow** in terms of covered persons; it applies to officers, directors, and key employees ONLY. Because Code Section 4958 does not apply to Code Section 501(c)(5), (6), or (7) organizations, no attempt is made to address persons who would be "disqualified persons" under Code Section 4958. Sample Policy B covers key employees using the definition from the Form 990 Instructions. This range of coverage may be appropriate for an organization that wishes to have in place a conflict of interest policy that meets the minimum requirements necessary to answer "Yes" to Lines 12a-c of Part VI.B, or an organization that wishes to have a separate conflict of interest policy that allows it to answer "Yes" to these questions, and separate policies that set forth the policy and procedure for dealing with the conflicts of interests of other persons (such as employees who are not key employees).

2. <u>Narrow Range of Covered Interests</u>. The policy is narrow in scope; it applies to material financial interests potentially affecting a person's judgment. Compliance with this Sample Policy B will not insure compliance with CCC Section 7233. The interests covered by this policy are potentially narrower. Some organizations may prefer a broader scope, focusing on all of the interests and transactions that are regulated by law.

3. <u>Covered Transactions and Relationships</u>. While the policy is designed to pick up many transactions and relationships to be disclosed on Form 990, it may not reach all

of them. An organization may need a more detailed disclosure form to collect all the information requested on other parts of current or future versions of Form 990.

4. <u>Disclosure of Family Relationships</u>. The form limits disclosure of family members to those presenting a specific potential conflict. Please be aware that the IRS *may* want names of all listed relatives. Be aware that, pending clarification by the IRS, not listing all relatives may not be sufficient disclosure to answer "Yes" to Part VI.B, Line 12c.

5. <u>Statutory Compliance Not Guaranteed</u>. Compliance with this sample policy ***does not guarantee compliance*** with all rules of law.

6. <u>The Board of Directors as Arbiter of Conflicts</u>. This sample policy assumes that the Board of Directors will be the arbiter of conflicts, and not a committee of the Board.

[NAME OF ORGANIZATION]

CONFLICT OF INTEREST POLICY[2]

Article I: Purpose

This conflict of interest policy is designed to foster public confidence in the integrity of **[Name of Organization]** (the "Organization") and to protect the Organization's interest when it is contemplating entering a transaction (defined below) that might benefit the private interest of a director, a corporate officer, the top management or top financial official, a key employee (defined below). [Note to Organization: Compliance with this Sample Policy B will not insure compliance with CCC Section 7233. The interests covered by this policy are potentially narrower.]

Article II: Definitions

The following are considered *insiders* for the purposes of this policy:

1. Each member of the Board of Directors or other governing body.

2. The president, chief executive officer, chief operating officer, treasurer and chief financial officer, executive director, or any person with the responsibilities of any of these positions (whether or not the person is an officer of the Organization under the Organization's Bylaws and the California Corporations Code).

---

[2] Note that this Conflict of Interest Policy does not assume the existence of a separate Compensation Policy. Compensation paid to insiders, including for their service as directors, officers, and key employees, should be evaluated under this Policy in its current form. If an organization has a separate Compensation Policy that addresses such compensation decisions, this sample policy may be modified accordingly.

3. Any *key employee*, meaning an employee whose total annual compensation (including benefits) from the organization and its affiliates is more than $150,000 **and** who (a) has responsibilities or influence over the organization similar to that of officers, directors, or trustees; **or** (b) manages a program that represents 10% or more of the activities, assets, income, or expenses of the organization; **or** (c) has or shares authority to control 10% or more of the organization's capital expenditures, operating budget, or compensation for employees.

Interest means any material financial interest, whether through commitment, investment, relationship, obligation, involvement or otherwise, direct or indirect, that may influence a person's judgment, including receipt of compensation from the Organization, a sale, loan, or exchange transaction with the Organization.

A *conflict of interest* is present when, in the judgment of the body or individual determining whether a conflict exists, an insider or person related to the insider by family or business relationship ("interested person") has a material financial interest in the transaction such that it reduces the likelihood that an insider's influence can be exercised impartially in the best interests of the Organization.

Transaction means any transaction, agreement, or arrangement between an interested person and the Organization, or between the Organization and any third party where an interested person has a material financial interest in the transaction or any party to it. [Note to Organization: If the Organization has a separate Compensation Policy that addresses the receipt of compensation by an insider in his or her capacity as an insider (e.g., compensation paid to the President for her services to the Organization as its President), please include the following sentence: "*Transaction* does not include compensation arrangements between the Organization and a director, officer, or other insider that are wholly addressed under the Organization's Compensation Policy."]

Article III: Procedures

1. *Duty to Disclose*

Each interested person shall disclose to the Board all material facts regarding his, her, or its interest (including relevant affiliations) in the transaction. The interested person shall make that disclosure promptly upon learning of the proposed transaction.

2. *Determining Whether a Conflict of Interest Exists*

With regard to an interested person, the Board shall determine if a conflict of interest exists.

3. *Procedures for Addressing a Conflict of Interest*

The Board shall follow the procedures set forth in Article IV in order to decide what measures are needed to protect the Organization's interests in light of the nature and seriousness of the conflict, to decide whether to enter into the transaction and, if so, to ensure that the terms of the transaction are appropriate. In the case of an insider who is a director, the director shall not vote on any transaction in which the director has an interest, and the remaining Board members shall decide the matter.

Article IV: Review by the Board

The Board may ask questions of and receive presentation(s) from the insider(s) and any other interested person(s), and may deliberate and vote on the transaction in their presence. The Board shall ascertain that all material facts regarding the transaction and the interested person's conflict of interest have been disclosed to the Board and shall compile appropriate data to ascertain whether the proposed transaction is just and reasonable to the Organization.

After exercising due diligence, which may include investigating alternatives that present no conflict, the Board shall determine whether the transaction is in the Organization's best interest, for its own benefit, and whether it is just and reasonable to the Organization; the transaction can be approved by the Board by majority vote of those present at a meeting for which quorum requirements have been met, without counting the vote of any interested directors. Interested or common directors may be counted in determining the presence of a quorum at such meeting.

Article V: Records of Proceedings

The minutes of any meeting of the Board pursuant to this policy shall contain the name of each interested person who disclosed or was otherwise determined to have an interest in a transaction; the nature of the interest and whether it was determined to constitute a conflict of interest; any alternative transactions considered; the members of the Board who were present during the debate on the transaction, those who voted on it, and to what extent interested persons were excluded from the deliberations; any comparability data or other information obtained and relied upon by the Board and how the information was obtained; and the result of the vote, including, if applicable, the terms of the transaction that was approved and the date it was approved.

Article VI: Annual Disclosure and Compliance Statements

Each director, each corporate officer, the top management official, the top financial official, and each key employee of the Organization, shall annually sign a statement on the form attached, that:

- affirms that the person has received a copy of this conflict of interest policy, has read and understood the policy, and has agreed to comply with the policy; and

- discloses the person's financial interests and family relationships that could give rise to conflicts of interest.

Article VII: Violations

If the Board has reasonable cause to believe that an insider of the Organization has failed to disclose actual or possible conflicts of interest, including those arising from a transaction with a related interested person, it shall inform such insider of the basis for this belief and afford the insider an opportunity to explain the alleged failure to disclose. If, after hearing the insider's response and making further investigation as warranted by the circumstances, the Board determines that the insider has failed to disclose an actual or possible conflict of interest, the Board shall take appropriate disciplinary and corrective action.

Article VIII: Annual Reviews

To ensure that the Organization operates in a manner consistent with its status as an organization exempt from federal income tax, the Board shall authorize and oversee an annual review of the administration of this conflict of interest policy. The review may be written or oral. The review shall consider the level of compliance with the policy, the continuing suitability of the policy, and whether the policy should be modified and improved.

[NAME OF ORGANIZATION]

CONFLICT OF INTEREST POLICY:
ACKNOWLEDGMENT AND FINANCIAL INTEREST DISCLOSURE STATEMENT

Our organization follows a conflict of interest policy designed to foster public confidence in our integrity and to protect our interest when we are contemplating entering a transaction or arrangement that might benefit the private interest of a director, a corporate officer, our top management official and top financial official, any of our key employees, or other interested persons.

Part I.   Acknowledgment of Receipt

> I hereby acknowledge that I have received a copy of the conflict of interest policy of **[NAME OF ORGANIZATION]**, have read and understood it, and agree to comply with its terms.
>
> _____   _____
> Signature   Date
>
> _____
> Printed Name

Part II. Disclosure of Financial Interests

We are required annually to file Form 990 with the Internal Revenue Service, and the form we file is available to the public. To complete Form 990 fully and accurately, we need each officer, director and key employee to disclose the information requested in this Part II.

A "conflict of interest," for purposes of Form 990, arises when a person in a position of authority over an organization, such as an officer, director, or key employee,

---

Part II Please check ONE of the following boxes:

☐ My interests and relationships have not changed since my last disclosure of interests. [Proceed to signature block below. Do not complete the tables.]

OR

☐ I hereby disclose or update my interests and relationships that could give rise to a conflict of interest: [Complete the table below. Use additional pages as needed.]

Family Relationships	Names of those presenting a potential conflict of interest
Include spouse/domestic partner, living ancestors, brothers and sisters (whether whole or half blood), children (whether natural or adopted), grandchildren, great grand-children, and spouses/ domestic partners of brothers, sisters, children, grandchildren, and great grandchildren	

Type of interest	Description of interest that could lead to a conflict of interest
Transactions or arrangements with the Organization	
Transactions or affiliations with other nonprofit organizations	
Substantial business or investment holdings	
Transactions or affiliations with businesses not listed above	

I am not aware of any financial interest involving me or a family member that could present a conflict of interest that I have not disclosed either above or in a previous disclosure statement.

_____   _____

may benefit financially from a decision he or she could make in such capacity, including indirect benefits such as to family members or businesses with which the person is closely associated.

C. *Sample Policy C: Code Section 501(c)(3) Organizations; Form 1023, Appendix A: Sample Conflict of Interest Policy.* The sample conflict of interest policy contained in Appendix A to the Instructions to the Form 1023 is flawed for many reasons, but because it was drafted by the Service and is included in the Form 1023 as a model policy, organizations should at least be familiar with its contents. The Instructions to Form 1023 were last updated in June 2006, prior to the revision of the new Form 990, so it is not clear that the Service considers the Appendix A policy to be sufficiently comprehensive to permit an organization to answer "Yes" to Lines 12a-c, for the reasons identified below. Note that Form 1023 and its sample Conflict of Interest Policy are only relevant to Code Section 501(c)(3) organizations.

1. No Annual Disclosure of Potential Conflicts of Interest. Line 12b of Part VI.B of the Form 990 asks if the organization requires "directors, officers, trustees, and key employees" to disclose annually any interests that good give rise to potential conflicts, including indirect conflicts created through family and business relationships. The Form 1023 sample Conflict of Interest Policy requires only that the directors, principal officers, and members of board committees annual acknowledge that they have read the organization's Conflict of Interest Policy and agreed to comply with it.

2. No Coverage of Key Employees. The Form 990 extends disclosure obligations to Key Employees, a concept that did not exist in the Form 990 when the sample policy in the Form 1023 was drafted. Therefore, in addition to not requiring annual disclosure of potential conflicts, the Form 1023 sample would not permit an organization to answer "Yes" to Line 12b of Part VI.B of the Form 990 because Line 12b asks about requirements for Key Employees.

3. Narrow Range of Covered Interests. The policy is narrow in scope, applying only to financial interests. Other types of interests that could give rise to conflicts are not covered.

4. <u>Federal and State Statutory Compliance Not Guaranteed</u>. Compliance with the Form 1023 sample policy ***does not guarantee compliance*** with Code Section 4958, Code Section 4941, or other applicable rules of law, including California state corporate law.

5. <u>Disclosure of Family Relationships</u>. The form does not require prior disclosure of business, investment, or family relationships, although it does treat as "financial interests" any interest created "directly or indirectly" through "business, investment, or family."

6. <u>Prior Transactions Not Addressed</u>. This policy does not address the approval process for past transactions that have already occurred or commenced.

Note: Items marked *Hospital insert – for hospitals that complete Schedule C* are intended to be adopted by hospitals.

Article I
Purpose

The purpose of the conflict of interest policy is to protect this tax-exempt organization's (Organization) interest when it is contemplating entering into a transaction or arrangement that might benefit the private interest of an officer or director of the Organization or might result in a possible excess benefit transaction. This policy is intended to supplement but not replace any applicable state and federal laws governing conflict of interest applicable to nonprofit and charitable organizations.

Article II
Definitions

1. Interested Person

Any director, principal officer, or member of a committee with governing board delegated powers, who has a direct or indirect financial interest, as defined below, is an interested person.

[Hospital Insert – for hospitals that complete Schedule C

If a person is an interested person with respect to any entity in the health care system of which the organization is a part, he or she is an interested person with respect to all entities in the health care system.]

2. Financial Interest

A person has a financial interest if the person has, directly or indirectly, through business, investment, or family:

    a. An ownership or investment interest in any entity with which the Organization has a transaction or arrangement,

    b. A compensation arrangement with the Organization or with any entity or individual with which the Organization has a transaction or arrangement, or

    c. A potential ownership or investment interest in, or compensation arrangement with, any entity or individual with which the Organization is negotiating a transaction or arrangement.

Compensation includes direct and indirect remuneration as well as gifts or favors that are not insubstantial.

A financial interest is not necessarily a conflict of interest. Under Article III, Section 2, a person who has a financial interest may have a conflict of interest only if the appropriate governing board or committee decides that a conflict of interest exists.

Article III
Procedures

1. Duty to Disclose

In connection with any actual or possible conflict of interest, an interested person must disclose the existence of the financial interest and be given the opportunity to disclose all material facts to the directors and members of committees with governing board delegated powers considering the proposed transaction or arrangement.

2. Determining Whether a Conflict of Interest Exists

After disclosure of the financial interest and all material facts, and after any discussion with the interested person, he/she shall leave the governing board or committee meeting while the determination of a conflict of interest is discussed and voted upon. The remaining board or committee members shall decide if a conflict of interest exists.

3. Procedures for Addressing the Conflict of Interest

a. An interested person may make a presentation at the governing board or committee meeting, but after the presentation, he/she shall leave the meeting during the discussion of, and the vote on, the transaction or arrangement involving the possible conflict of interest.

b. The chairperson of the governing board or committee shall, if appropriate, appoint a disinterested person or committee to investigate alternatives to the proposed transaction or arrangement.

c. After exercising due diligence, the governing board or committee shall determine whether the Organization can obtain with reasonable efforts a more advantageous transaction or arrangement from a person or entity that would not give rise to a conflict of interest.

d. If a more advantageous transaction or arrangement is not reasonably possible under circumstances not producing a conflict of interest, the governing board or committee shall determine by a majority vote of the disinterested directors whether the transaction or arrangement is in the Organization's best interest, for its own benefit, and whether it is fair and reasonable. In conformity with the above determination it shall make its decision as to whether to enter into the transaction or arrangement.

4. **Violations of the Conflicts of Interest Policy**

   a. If the governing board or committee has reasonable cause to believe a member has failed to disclose actual or possible conflicts of interest, it shall inform the member of the basis for such belief and afford the member an opportunity to explain the alleged failure to disclose.

   b. If, after hearing the member's response and after making further investigation as warranted by the circumstances, the governing board or committee determines the member has failed to disclose an actual or possible conflict of interest, it shall take appropriate disciplinary and corrective action.

Article IV
Records of Proceedings

The minutes of the governing board and all committees with board delegated powers shall contain:

   a. The names of the persons who disclosed or otherwise were found to have a financial interest in connection with an actual or possible conflict of interest, the nature of the financial interest, any action taken to determine whether a conflict of interest was present, and the governing board's or committee's decision as to whether a conflict of interest in fact existed.

   b. The names of the persons who were present for discussions and votes relating to the transaction or arrangement, the content of the discussion, including any alternatives to the proposed transaction or arrangement, and a record of any votes taken in connection with the proceedings.

Article V
Compensation

a. A voting member of the governing board who receives compensation, directly or indirectly, from the Organization for services is precluded from voting on matters pertaining to that member's compensation.

b. A voting member of any committee whose jurisdiction includes compensation matters and who receives compensation, directly or indirectly, from the Organization for services is precluded from voting on matters pertaining to that member's compensation.

c. No voting member of the governing board or any committee whose jurisdiction includes compensation matters and who receives compensation, directly or indirectly, from the Organization, either individually or collectively, is prohibited from providing information to any committee regarding compensation.

[*Hospital Insert – for hospitals that complete Schedule C*

d. Physicians who receive compensation from the Organization, whether directly or indirectly or as employees or independent contractors, are precluded from membership on any committee whose jurisdiction includes compensation matters. No physician, either individually or collectively, is prohibited from providing information to any committee regarding physician compensation.]

Article VI
Annual Statements

Each director, principal officer and member of a committee with governing board delegated powers shall annually sign a statement which affirms such person:

a. Has received a copy of the conflicts of interest policy,

b. Has read and understands the policy,

c. Has agreed to comply with the policy, and

d. Understands the Organization is charitable and in order to maintain its federal tax exemption it must engage primarily in activities which accomplish one or more of its tax-exempt purposes.

Article VII
Periodic Reviews

To ensure the Organization operates in a manner consistent with charitable purposes and does not engage in activities that could jeopardize its tax-exempt status, periodic reviews shall be conducted. The periodic reviews shall, at a minimum, include the following subjects:

a. Whether compensation arrangements and benefits are reasonable, based on competent survey information, and the result of arm's length bargaining.

b. Whether partnerships, joint ventures, and arrangements with management organizations conform to the Organization's written policies, are properly recorded, reflect reasonable investment or payments for goods and services, further charitable purposes and do not result in inurement, impermissible private benefit or in an excess benefit transaction.

Article VIII
Use of Outside Experts

When conducting the periodic reviews as provided for in Article VII, the Organization may, but need not, use outside advisors. If outside experts are used, their use shall not relieve the governing board of its responsibility for ensuring periodic reviews are conducted.

Credit: Public Counsel Law Center
Credit: www.councilofnonprofits.org

(I want to thank www.northwestregisteredagent.com, **Public Counsel Law Center and** www.councilofnonprofits.org **for their vast information on NPO. I urge every reader to visit these sites for up-to-date information along with many other relevant material)**

Made in the USA
Las Vegas, NV
11 October 2023

78932284R00201